The Tauiwi

The Later Immigrants

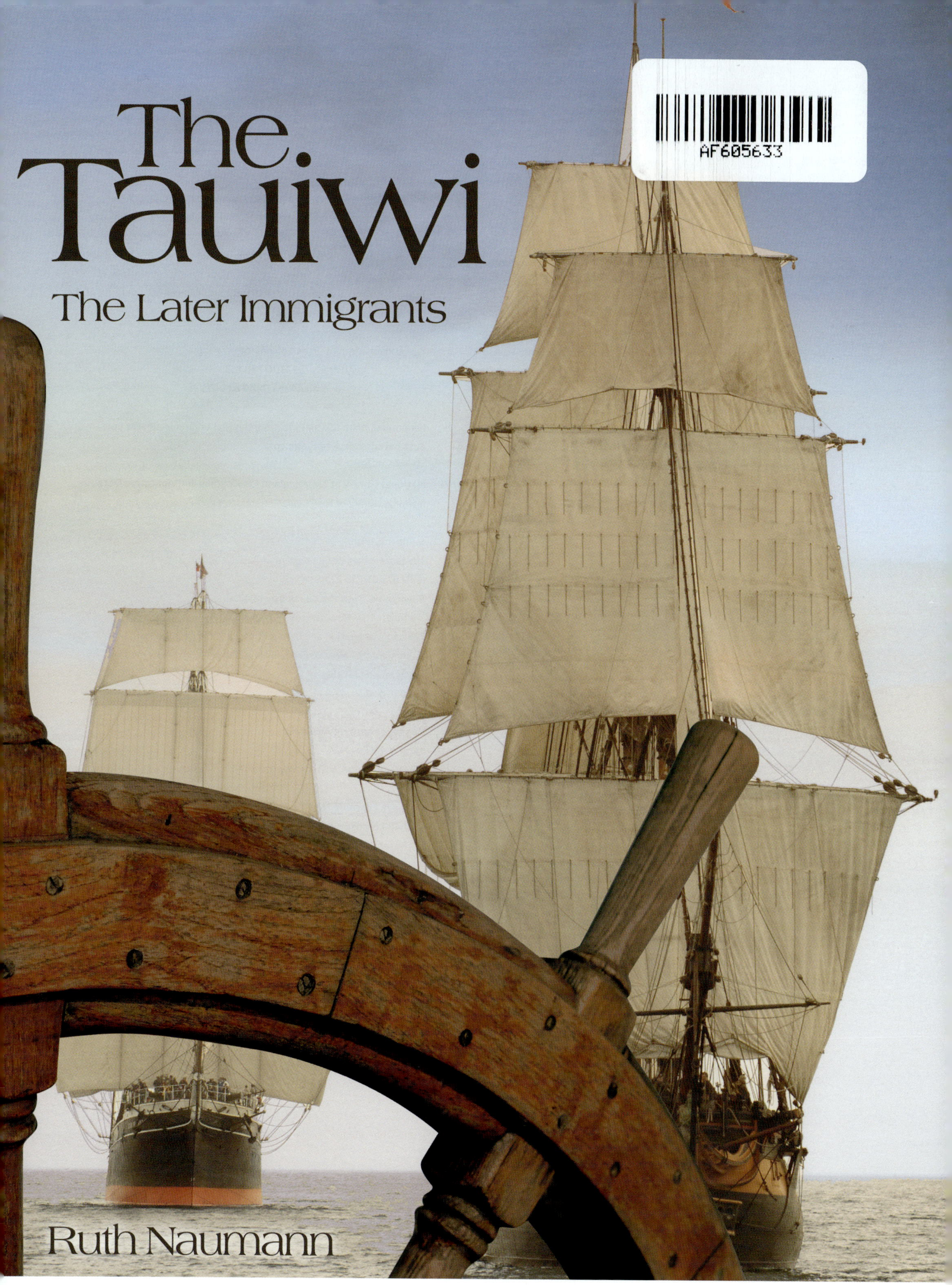

Ruth Naumann

NELSON CENGAGE Learning™

Australia • Brazil • Japan • Korea • Mexico • Singapore • Spain • United Kingdom • United States

The Tauiwi: The Later Immigrants
2nd Edition
Ruth Naumann

Text and cover design: Cheryl Rowe, Macarn Design
Typeset: Cheryl Rowe, Macarn Design
Production controller: Siew Han Ong
Reprint: Jess Lovell

Any URLs contained in this publication were checked for currency during the production process. Note, however, that the publisher cannot vouch for the ongoing currency of URLs.

First published as *The Tauiwi* by New House Publishers in 1990.

Acknowledgements

Laurence Clark for illustrations on pages 10-13, 17, 20, 29 and 30. The New Zealand Herald for the photograph of Danny Lee on page 52. The Hocken Collection (University of Otago) for the photograph on page 15. Shutterstock for cover images and photographs on pages 5, 47 and 53. Istock for photograph of Amber on pg 31. The following images are courtesy of Alexander Turnball Library, Wellington, New Zealand: Page 5: Working Men's Educational Union:[View of Dunedin. 1862]. London, Working Men's Educational Union, Reference No. D-010-012; Page 9 (top): Wivell, Abraham 1786-1849: Edward Gibbon Wakefield, Esq. Engraved by B Holl from a drawing by A Wivell, 1823. London, 1826, Reference No. A-042-023; Page 9 (bottom): Punch :The needlewoman at home and abroad. [London, 1850], Reference No. PUBL -0043-1850-01; Page 12: Calvert, Samuel, ca 1828-1913: The burning of the emigrant ship Cospatrick off the Cape of Good Hope [1874]. Auckland, Illustrated New Zealand Herald, 1875. Reference No. PUBL-0047-1875-09; Page 14: [Weld, Frederick Aloysius] 1823-1891: [Lyttelton, with Immigrants' Barracks and settlers' houses, 1852?], Reference No. B-139-004; Page 16 (top): Shop of A. Harris, saddler, in Reefton, 1897, Reference No. 1/2-151909-F; Page 16: (bottom): Men working in a blacksmithing shop [ca 1910], Reference No. PAColl-5521-18; Page 19: Mesopotamia Station, showing house, group and surrounding land, 1871, Reference No. MNZ-0386-1/4-F; Page 21 (top): Panning for gold, West Coast [189-?], Reference No. 1/2-044390-F; Page 21 (bottom): Ring, James, 1856-1939: Photograph of gold sluicing at Dillman Town, West Coast [188-?], Reference No. PAColl-8654; Page 23 (top): Artist unknown: Pipes for the gold diggings at J. Inderwick's, wholesale and retail warehouse, [1850s?], Reference No. C-038-016; Page 23 (bottom right): Advertisement for Spicer and Murray, undertakers, from Harnett's Directory, 1866, Reference No. 1/2-031932-F; Page 24: Chinese gold miner with cradle, on the banks of the Clutha River, between November 1900 and February 1901, Reference No. 1/2-019695-F; Page 28 (left): Gum digging village, ca 1910, Reference No. 1/1-006280-G; Page 28 (middle): Photograph of Liza Tahi; Ca 1910, Reference No. 1/2 -066527-F; Page 28 (right): Group gum digging, between ca 1910 - ca 1939, Reference No. 1/2-038717-F; Page 33: Group watching a boxing match on a gum field, Ca 1912, Reference No. 1/1-011205-G; Page 34 (left): Group outside a timber camp hut [ca 1900], Reference No. PA1-o-395-05; Page 34 (right): Scene in the bush showing a thatched hut, three people, and washing on a line, ca 1860s, Reference No. 1/2-004135-F; Page 36 (top): Lawrence, Charles L (Christchurch) fl 1872-1878: Portrait of Mrs Cridland and a young child, [between 1867-1879], Reference No. PA2-0992; Page 36 (bottom): Women vote at their first election, Tahakopa, 1893, Reference No. PA1-o-550-34-1; Page 41 (top): Looking through native bush, over the area near to the Puhoi river mouth, between 1863-1905, Reference No. 1/2-096239-G; Page 41: Puhoi township and school, [Between 1900 and 1930], Reference No. 1/2-000153-G; Page 42 (top): Strutt, William 1825-1915 :Underbrushing. New Zealand forest. [1844 or 1856]; Reference No. E-453-f -012-4; Page 42 (bottom): [Blomfield, Charles] 1848-1926: [Bush hut. 1880s?], Reference No. G-375; Page 43: Strutt, William 1825-1915: Bush falling, Taranaki, New Zealand. Jan., 1857, Reference No. E-453-f-010; Page 44: Bush camp, [ca 1910], Reference No. 1/2 -024134-G; Page 46 (top): The ruined buildings along the main street of Hebuterne, France, 12 May 1918, Reference No. 1/2-013191-G; Page 46 (bottom): Artist and pianist Martin Roestenburg, and his family, in Wellington after arriving on a Dutch immigrant ship, 28 Sep 1951, Reference No. 114/362/10-G; Page 48 (left): Children at the Polish refugee camp in Pahiatua, 1945, Reference No. 1/2-003659-F; Page 48 (right): Cambodian refugees learning to ride bicycles in Waikanae - Photograph taken by Melanie Burford, 29 November 1995, Reference No. EP/1995/4608/6-F; Page 50: The 'occasionally' Pacific Islands. 20 November, 2006. Reference No. DCDL-0002695; Page 52 (top): Taranaki business man Chew Chong, [191-?], Reference No. 1/2-023954-F; Page 52 (bottom left): Photograph taken by Brent Carryer, 20 September 2002-21 September 2002, Reference No. PADL-000011; Page 52 (bottom middle): Chinese dragon being carried across a pedestrian crossing, Wellington - Photograph taken by Craig Simcox, 18 September 1999, Reference No. EP/1999/2748/17; Page 53: 'Peter Brown, NZ First Deputy Leader, suggests door be shut on Asian migrants - News'. "One Thai green curry for Mister Brown - COMING UP!" 10 April, 2008, Reference No. DCDL-0006010; Page 54: Crowd on the beach at Caroline Bay, Timaru - Photograph taken by William Ferrier, [ca 1890], Reference No. PAColl-4746-02; Page 55 (left): Migrant investors with $20 million to be allowed residence without English language skills - News. "G'day mate, I used to be married to an old chook at the back of Bourke but decided to do a waltzing Matilda before I carked it." "He must be worth a few bob." 7 June, 2007, Reference No. DCDL-0003389; Page 55 (right): Boy with a penny farthing bicycle - Photographer unidentified, ca 1880s, Reference No. MNZ-0604-1/4-F.

For product information and technology assistance,
in Australia call **1300 790 853**;
in New Zealand call **0800 449 725**

For permission to use material from this text or product, please email
aust.permissions@cengage.com

National Library of New Zealand Cataloguing-in-Publication Data
National Library of New Zealand Cataloguing-in-Publication Data

Naumann, Ruth.
The tauiwi : the later immigrants / Ruth Naumann. 2nd ed.
ISBN 978-017018-225-6
Previous ed.: New House Publishers, 1990.
1. Immigrants—New Zealand—Juvenile literature. 2. New Zealand—Emigration and immigration—Juvenile literature.
[1. Immigrants—New Zealand. 2. New Zealand—Emigration and immigration.] I. Title.
325.93—dc 22

Cengage Learning Australia

South Melbourne, Victoria Australia 3205

Cengage Learning New Zealand
Unit 4B Rosedale Office Park
331 Rosedale Road, Albany, North Shore 0632, NZ

For learning solutions, visit **cengage.co.nz**

Printed in Australia by Ligare Pty Limited.
5 6 7 8 9 10 11 19 18 17 16 15

Contents

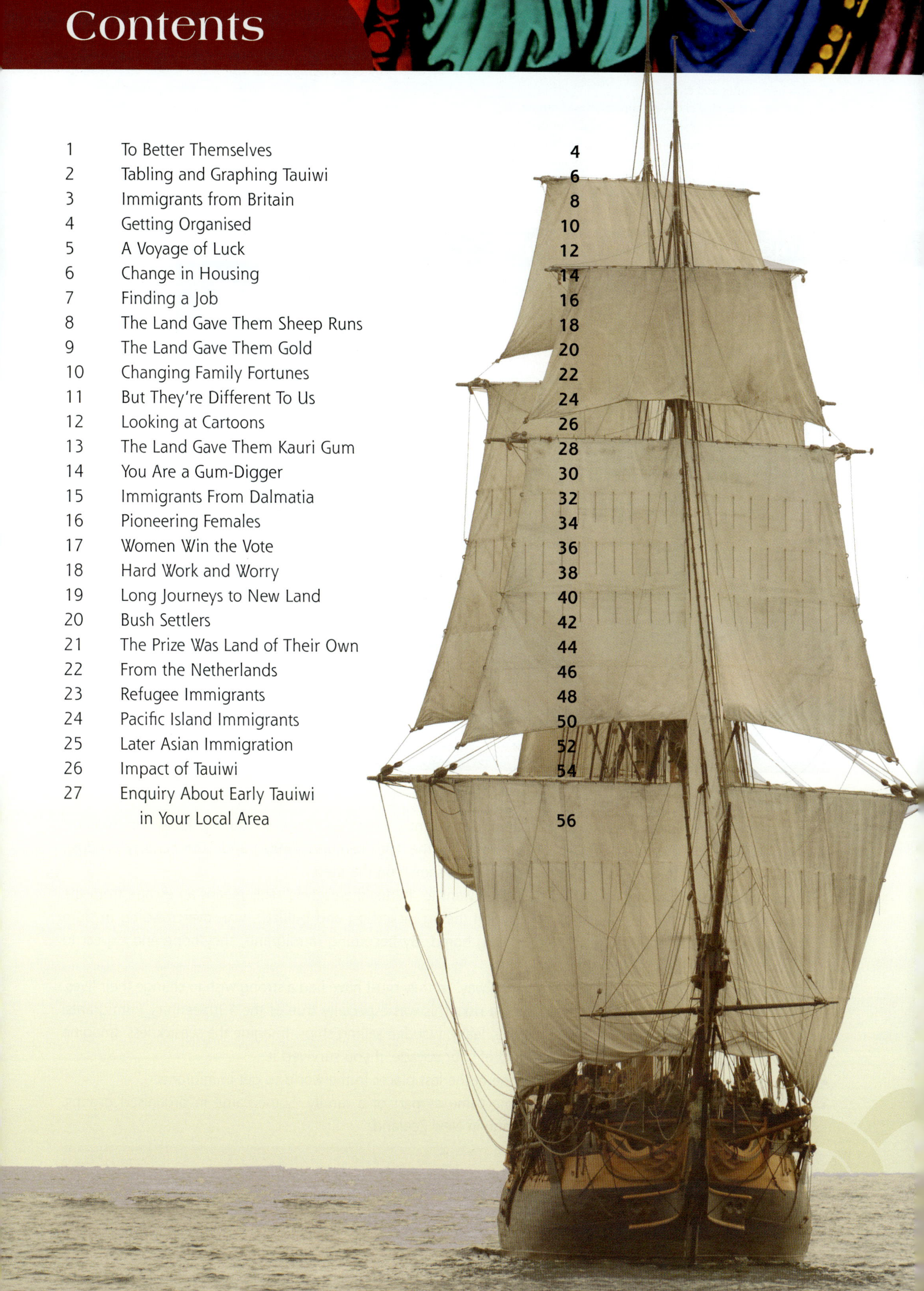

To Better Themselves

Focus

- Events have causes and effects.
- People respond to challenges as individuals and groups.
- People move between places which has results for people and places.
- Ideas and actions of people in the past helped shape society.
- Economic decisions have an impact on people and communities.
- The way people manage resources has an impact on the environment.

Immigration to New Zealand

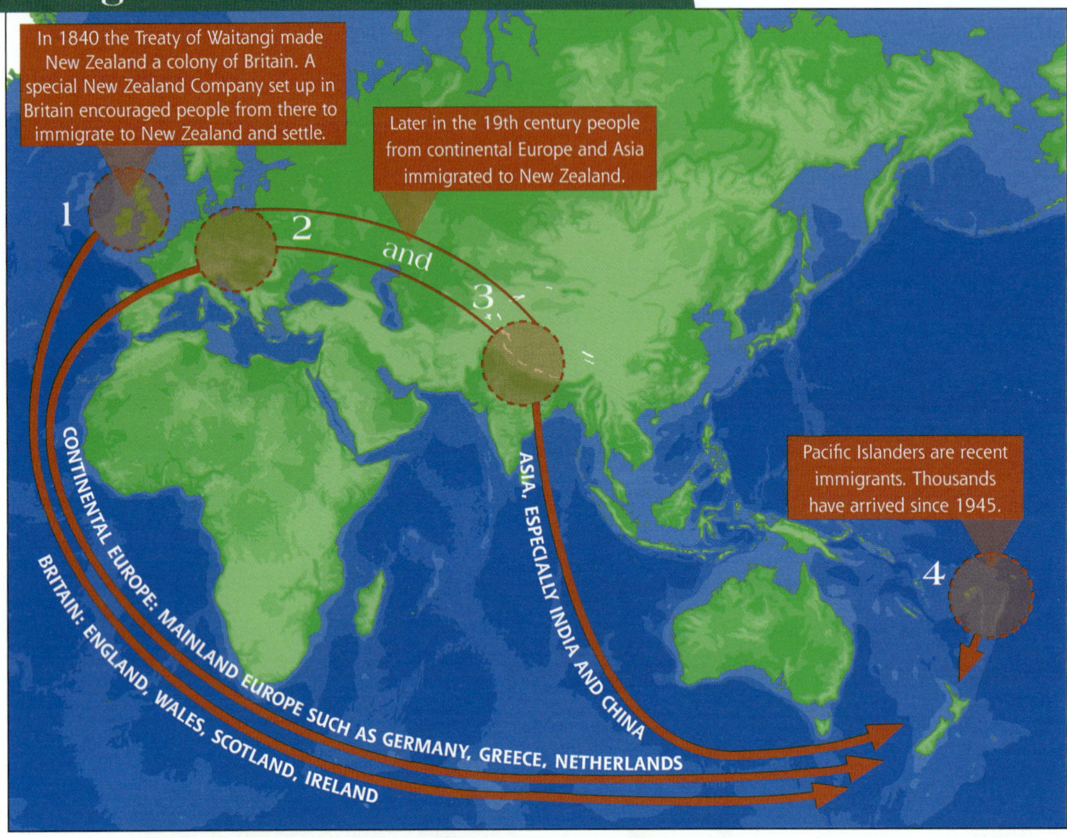

Some important points to do with the map are:

- Immigrants are travellers. They travel from their own country to settle in another country. Today's immigrants come to New Zealand from all parts of the world. In the 19th century (1800s) and 20th century (1900s), immigrants tended to come from the four main areas shown on the map.
- People become immigrants mainly because they want to 'better themselves'. This means an escape from the negative things in their lives such as persecution (being picked on and bullied), war, overcrowding in slum housing, having no job, having no land, feeling bored. By becoming immigrants, they hope and expect to bring more positive things into their lives.
- Immigrants to New Zealand had to travel a long way. So they must have had a strong wish to change their lives. They must also have been brave to take such a risk. This was especially true of the 19th century immigrants. They spent months crossing the ocean in small, leaky, wooden sailing ships. Imagine the seasickness. Imagine not knowing what would greet you at the end of your voyage, if you survived it.
- New Zealand is isolated. This meant it was one of the last places in the world to get immigrants.
- Some immigrants came by themselves. Some came as part of a family. Some came in organised groups. Because so many came they accelerated change in New Zealand.

These later immigrants have been called Tauiwi.
Tauiwi means 'strange tribe' or 'foreign race' – people different to the known Maori tribes.
Tauiwi have had great impact.

ISBN 9780170182256

They changed how the environment looked

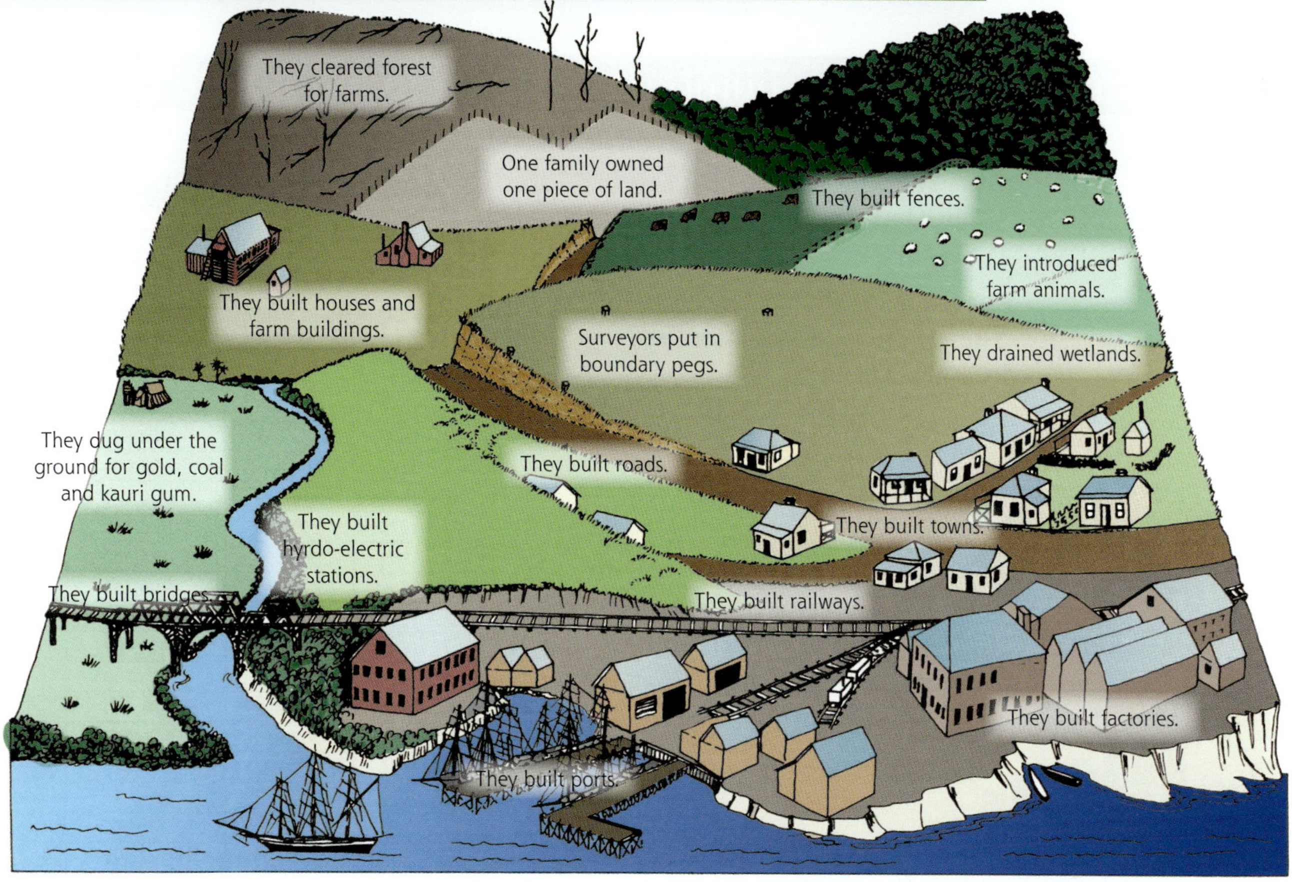

They cleared forest for farms.

One family owned one piece of land.

They built fences.

They introduced farm animals.

They built houses and farm buildings.

Surveyors put in boundary pegs.

They drained wetlands.

They dug under the ground for gold, coal and kauri gum.

They built roads.

They built hyrdo-electric stations.

They built towns.

They built bridges.

They built railways.

They built factories.

They built ports.

Activities

1 Describe the link between the Treaty of Waitangi and the beginning of organised immigration to New Zealand.

2 Explain the difference between iwi and Tauiwi.

3 Describe what people meant in the 19th century when they said they were coming to New Zealand in order to 'better themselves'.

4 Research: Find five graphics that illustrate one of the changes to the environment that Tauiwi made in the 19th century.

ISBN 9780170182256

Tabling and Graphing Tauiwi

Focus

- Events have causes and effects.
- People respond to challenges as individuals and groups.
- People move between places which has results for people and places.
- Ideas and actions of people in the past helped shape society.

Immigrants changed the number of people living on the land.

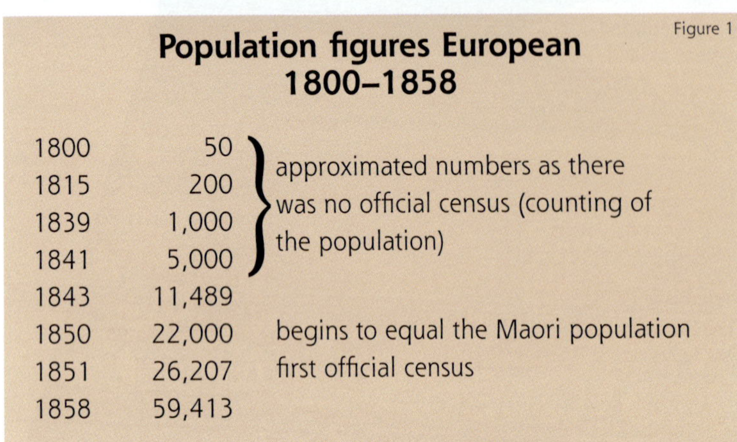

Figure 1

Population figures European 1800–1858

1800	50	approximated numbers as there was no official census (counting of the population)
1815	200	
1839	1,000	
1841	5,000	
1843	11,489	
1850	22,000	begins to equal the Maori population
1851	26,207	first official census
1858	59,413	

Figure 2

100 years of immigrants

Contribution of Immigrants to Non-Maori Population, 1861–1961

Census	Persons Born Overseas	Persons Born in New Zealand
1861	68,496	26,487
1864	129,781	40,086
1867	153,847	62,820
1871	162,379	92,009
1874	176,373	120,775
1878	239,388	172,179
1881	265,696	221,360
1886	276,263	298,232
1891	258,925	364,532
1896	261,095	439,402
1901	256,171	513,700
1906	281,859	603,669
1911	304,910	699,900
1916	303,702	790,918
1921	311,977	902,047
1926	323,955	991,296
1936	291,833	1,197,591
1945	245,183	1,357,323
1951	265,242	1,557,286
1956	309,547	1,726,193
1961	338,673	1,907,423

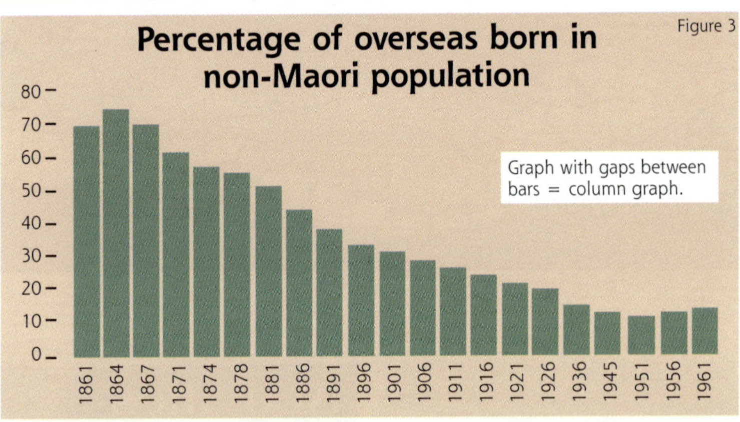

Figure 3

Percentage of overseas born in non-Maori population

Immigrants changed New Zealand's relationship with the rest of the world by setting up a trade economy. This means they exported goods from New Zealand and imported goods from other countries, especially Britain. This influenced immigration.

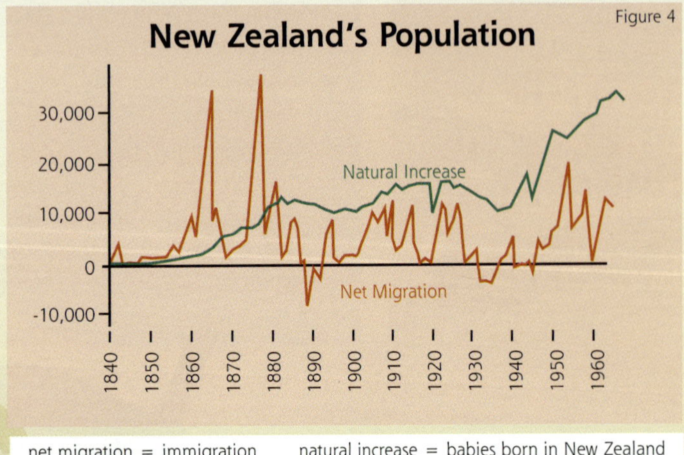

Figure 4

New Zealand's Population

net migration = immigration natural increase = babies born in New Zealand

Figure 5

	Immigration	Changes
1	early 1840s	first groups of organised immigrants
2	mid 1840s	economic depression
3	1860s	gold rushes
4	end of 60s	economic depression
5	1870s	Government immigration schemes
6	1880s	refrigeration
7	late 80s	economic depression
8	1900–1914	Government immigration schemes
9	1914–1918	World War I
10	1919–1926	Government immigration schemes
11	1930s	economic depression
12	1939–1945	World War II

ISBN 9780170182256

Immigrants changed the ancestral homeland of the majority people.

For centuries, the first immigrants had been the only people. They had spoken of Hawaiki, a Polynesian ancestral homeland. Now the majority spoke of Britain as being Home.

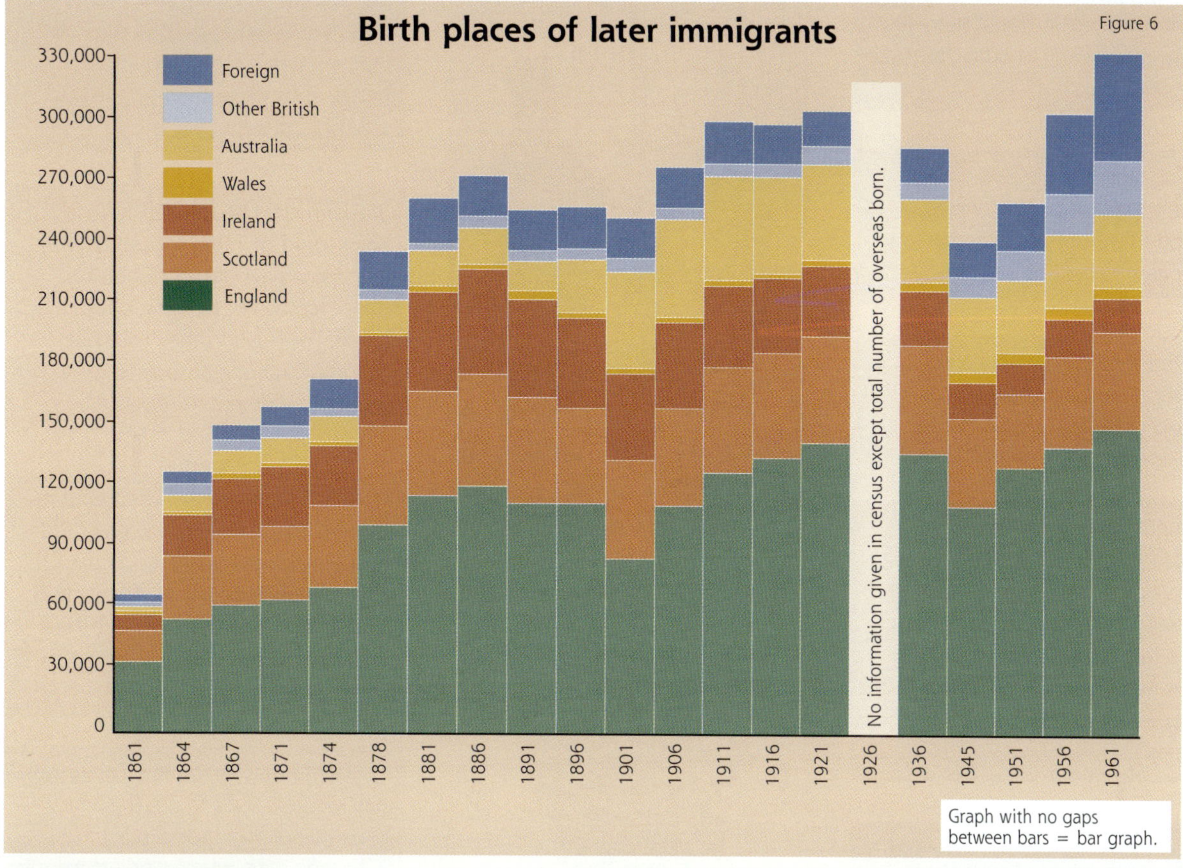

Activities

1 Put the population figures in Figure 1 on to either a bar or line graph.

2 The table and graph (Figures 2 and 3) used the same statistics but showed them in different ways. Explain the differences. Describe any advantages or disadvantages of each way.

3 Refer to Figure 5. Draw up a 3 column chart like the one below. Your chart will have 12 lines for you to fill in, using the symbols provided.

Time	Immigration change	Reason

Symbols

Immigration changes: increase ∧, decrease ∨

Reasons

O organised groups **G** government
D depression **Go** gold
R refrigeration **W** war

4 Today the selection of new immigrants is based on 'personal merit without discrimination on grounds of race, national or ethnic origin, colour, sex or marital status, religion or ethical belief'. However, for a long time the main emphasis was on getting immigrants from Britain. Explain how the graph (Figure 6) shows this.

5 Make your own copy of years 1861, 1875, 1921 and 1945 from the graph (Figure 6). Colour code it: red = immigrants from Britain, green = immigrants from other countries.

6 Start a Glossary for your Tauiwi study. A glossary is a list of special words with their technical meanings eg. depression = drop in business activity.

7 Research: Find five graphics you could use to illustrate the statistics in this unit.

ISBN 9780170182256

Settlers From Britain

Focus
- Events have causes and effects.
- People respond to challenges as individuals and groups.
- Ideas and actions of people in the past helped shape society.

There were strong class groups. If you were born into the working class only a miracle would see you moving up into the middle class or the upper class.

Working class people had no say in changing things. They were not allowed to vote in parliamentary elections.

Only the wealthy got educated. In 1842, one third of people in England could not read or write.

During the Industrial Revolution people invented machines to do jobs such as spinning and weaving. They set machines up in factories. Before this, workers at home had done these jobs by hand. Now they had to shift into towns to work in factories.

People, including children, worked long hours in factories with few windows to give light and air. Working with machines was dangerous. There were no laws about things like minimum wages. There were no trade unions to make conditions better.

Working class people lived in poor conditions in towns. Houses were overcrowded. They were jammed together in rows with no trees or gardens. There were no proper drains, water supplies or electricity. Diseases did well. Crime rose.

Children of working class parents often died before they reached five. Some children worked in coal mines pulling carts along narrow tunnels. Some were chimney sweeps. Some were beggars. Some stole to help feed their families.

Working class people were poor. There were no government hand-outs. You could end up in the Poor House. People said it would be better to be dead than go to such a terrible place.

Working class people felt hopeless. They could be hung for things like burning a haystack or disguising their faces when carrying out a crime. For stealing they could be put in prison or transported off to a convict settlement in Australia.

Only the upper class owned land in Britain. The chance of owning land of their own was the most powerful magnet for immigrants. Agents told people they only had to tickle New Zealand soil and things would start to grow.

On farms, machines were doing jobs that workers used to do. In some places workers attacked machines with their axes. Many workers were thrown off the land. Workers left to look for jobs in towns. This meant more overcrowding.

Some middle class and upper class people became immigrants because they wanted adventure. Others had families who sent them money to stay away.

Religion was important in society at this time. Religious arguments sometimes split churches. One happened in Scotland in 1843. People wanted to set up a new Church in a new land. Some immigrants thought of themselves as pilgrims. They said New Zealand was the Promised Land.

ISBN 9780170182256

In 1827 an Englishman called Edward Gibbon Wakefield began a three-year stretch in a London prison. His crime was abducting (kidnapping) a 15-year-old heiress. He had tricked her into leaving school by telling her a lie about her mother. Edward had ideas about immigration to New Zealand. He used his time in prison to get these down on paper.

- Land will be bought from Maori and then sold at a higher price to wealthy English people.
- Profits from the sale of land will pay for fares of labourers.
- The price of land must be high enough so that labourers will not be able to afford to buy it for some years. They will have to work to save money. This will mean plenty of labour for farmers.
- Immigrants must set up small farms like those in England. Each farming village will have things like schools and churches.

It sounded fine on paper. A group of wealthy men formed an organisation called the New Zealand Company. It brought about 12,000 immigrants to New Zealand in the next ten years. It offered assisted immigration. For example, it gave free travel to mechanics, gardeners and agricultural labourers.

Many people in Britain had never heard of New Zealand. To get them interested, the Company advertised in 52 centres. The Company paid immigration agents for every migrant they enrolled. Agents had to work hard to convince people that New Zealand was not full of blood-thirsty cannibals and escaped convicts from Australia.

Agents used leaflets like this.

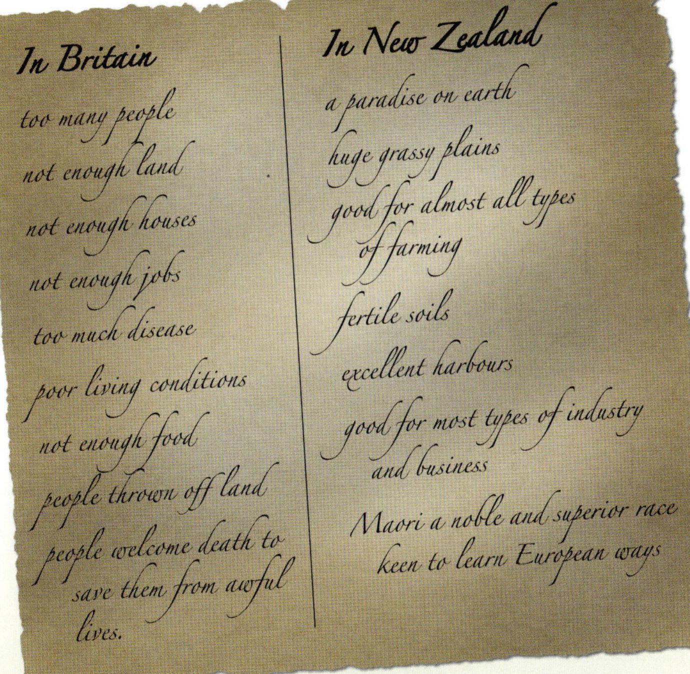

In Britain	*In New Zealand*
too many people	a paradise on earth
not enough land	huge grassy plains
not enough houses	good for almost all types of farming
not enough jobs	fertile soils
too much disease	excellent harbours
poor living conditions	good for most types of industry and business
not enough food	Maori a noble and superior race keen to learn European ways
people thrown off land	
people welcome death to save them from awful lives.	

HERE AND THERE; OR, EMIGRATION A REMEDY.

Activities

1. Explain why and how Britain was different to New Zealand in 1840.
2. Discuss why Wakefield's ideas might have sounded good on paper but that did not mean they were going to work in New Zealand.
3. Make a poster to advertise New Zealand to British people in 1840.
4. Research: Find out more about the British class system of this time.

ISBN 9780170182256

Getting Organised

Focus

- Events have causes and effects.
- People respond to challenges as individuals and groups.
- People move between places which has results for people and places.

If you were an immigration agent you would tell people who wanted to be assisted immigrants that they should, as a general rule,

- belong to the working classes
- be fit enough to work in New Zealand
- be a married couple
- be a young couple with no children
- have no more than two children under seven years old
- not be older than 40
- be under the care of married relatives of upper class cabin passengers, if they are single females
- be able to produce a marriage certificate
- have been vaccinated or have had the smallpox
- be able to supply their own blankets, sheets, towels, soap, knives, forks, tin or pewter plates, spoons, drinking mugs
- be able to supply their own clothes to be checked at port by a company officer
- be allowed to keep the mattresses and bolsters (pillows) provided by the ship when they arrive in New Zealand, if they behave themselves on the voyage.

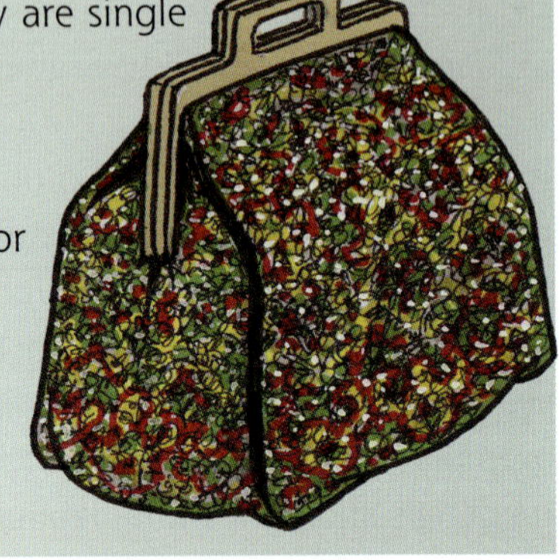

Your Food Allowances

NEW ZEALAND COMPANY — STEERAGE DIETARY

FOR EACH PERSON FOURTEEN YEARS OLD AND UPWARDS.

	Prime India Beef.	Prime Mess Pork.	Preserved Meat.	Biscuit.	Flour.	Rice.	Preserved Potatoes.	Peas.	Oatmeal.	Raisins.	Suet.	Butter.	Sugar.	Tea.	Coffee.	Salt.	Pepper.	Mustard.	Vinegar or Pickles.	Water.
	lb.	lb.	lb.	lb.	lb.	lb.	lb.	pint	One Pint Weekly.	Eight Ounces Weekly.	Four Ounces Weekly.	Eight Ounces Weekly.	Sixteen Ounces Weekly.	Two Ounces Weekly.	Two Ounces Weekly.	Two Ounces Weekly.	A Quarter-Ounce Weekly.	Half-an-Ounce Weekly.	Half-a-Pint Weekly	quarts
Sunday......	—	—	½	¾	¼	—	¼	—												3
Monday.....	—	½	—	¾	¼	—	—	¼												3
Tuesday.....	½	—	—	¾	¼	¼	—	—												3
Wednesday ..	—	—	½	¾	¼	—	¼	—												3
Thursday	—	½	—	¾	¼	—	—	¼												3
Friday	—	—	½	¾	¼	—	¼	—												3
Saturday	½	—	—	¾	¼	¼	—	—												3
Total Weekly	1 lb.	1 lb.	1½ lb.	5¼ lbs.	1¾ lbs.	½ lb.	¾ lbs.	½ pint	1 pint	8 oz.	4 oz.	8 oz.	16 oz.	2 oz.	2 oz.	2 oz.	¼ oz.	½ oz.	½ pint.	21 qrts.

Children Seven Years old and under Fourteen receive each, of Water, three Pints a day ; of other Articles, *Five-Eighths* of the Ration of an Adult.

Children One Year old and under Seven receive each, of Water, three Pints a day ; of Preserved Milk, a Quarter-Pint a day ; and of other Articles, Three-Eighths of an Adult Ration ; or, if directed by the Surgeon, either Four Ounces of Rice or Three Ounces of Sago, in lieu of Salt Meat, three time a week.

Infants under One Year old do not receive any Ration ; but the Surgeon is empowered to direct an Allowance of Water, for their use, to be issued to their Mothers. No charge is made for their Passage.

The several Articles of Diet may be varied from time to time, under the direction of the Surgeon, so as to promote the health and comfort of the Passengers, especially of Children.

New Zealand House, 9 Broad Street Buildings,
London, 1st November, 1848.

ration = amount allowed
surgeon = doctor
in lieu of = instead of
sago = starchy food stuff used to make puddings

1 oz (ounce) = 28.4g
1 lb (pound) = 453.6g
1 pt (pint) = 570 ml
1 qrt (quart) = 2 pints

Your Clothing Requirements

FEMALE

- 2 Gowns
- 2 Petticoats
- 12 Shirts
- 6 Caps
- 6 Handkerchiefs
- 6 Aprons
- 6 Neckerchiefs
- 6 Towels
- 1 Pair stays
- 6 Pair black stockings
- 2 Pair shoes

MALE

- 2 Jackets
- 2 Pair Trousers
- 2 Smocks
- 12 Shirts
- 6 Pair stockings
- 2 Caps
- 6 Handkerchiefs
- 6 Towels
- 1 Pair boots
- 1 Pair shoes

ISBN 9780170182256

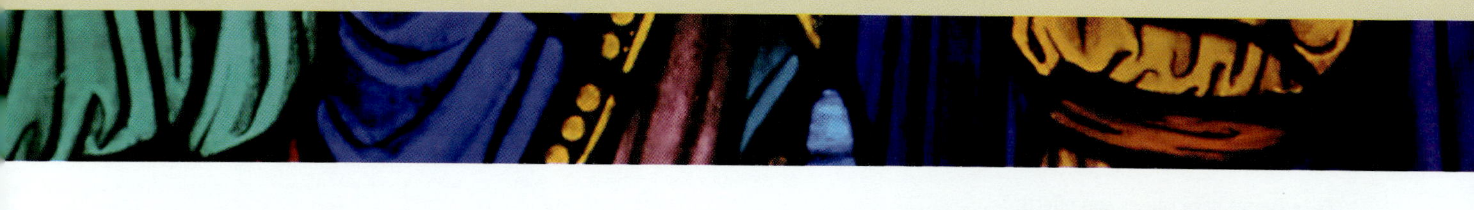

Many British people in the 1840s had lived all their lives in one village. They had never been to the next village 10km or less away. Yet here they were planning to travel around the world to live in a new place. They knew they would probably never see their home country or family and friends again.

This poem comes from the diary kept by Eliza Vosper when she sailed out to New Zealand from Plymouth in England. Her voyage on the sailing ship *Piako* lasted five months. In those days it was not unusual for people to put their feelings into verse.

My Mother's Parting Gift

The moon was fair and friends were
  gathered,
To wish me a long good-bye,
And as I kissed my mother darling
A starting tear stood in her eye.
She gave to me a lock of hair,
And from that lock I n'er will part,
It was my mother's parting gift,
I'll always wear it near my heart.

If I return she may be sleeping
With my father in his grave,
May all good angels watch and keep him,
And my tender mother save.
Though distant lands and sea divides us
I will think of her both night and day
There is no love like a dear mother,
We miss her when she is far away.

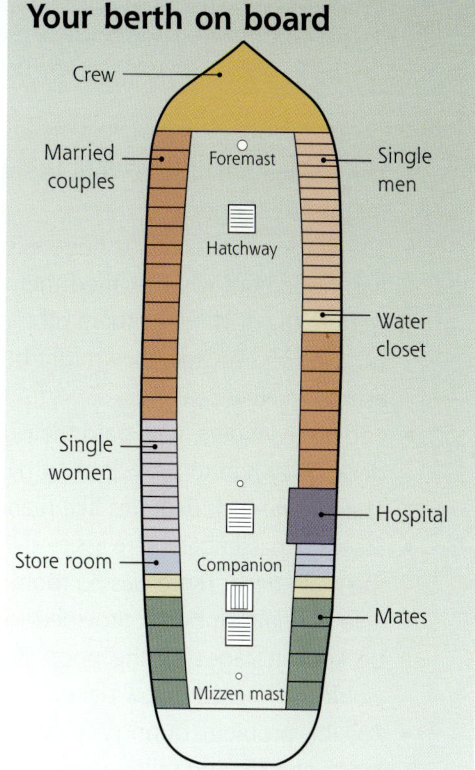

Activities

1 Make up a poem about leaving for New Zealand. Try to put in some positive, exciting things about your future.

2 As an immigration agent, make a decision about the eight people and families below who want to be assisted immigrants. Show your decisions on a chart.

The Redford family:

husband = 35, brick-maker;
wife = 34;
children = 12, 9, 6, 5, 4, 2, 1.

Laura:

18, single, works as domestic servant to family who intend going to NZ as cabin passengers.

John:

40, single, lace-maker.

The Waters family:

husband = 27, shepherd;
wife = 25;
children = 7, 5, 2.

The Bryd family:

husband = 39, unemployed, lost arm in accident;
wife = 35, takes in washing, no children.

Henry:

16, agricultural mechanic's apprentice.

The Leed family:

husband = 21, farm labourer;
wife = 20;
children = 3, 1.

The Paul family:

husband = 36, widower, gardener;
children = 16, 14, 12, 11, 10, 7.

Name	Yes/No	Reason for decision	Commission Yes/No
Redford family			

3 As an immigrant, draw your bag and trunk and say what you have packed in each. You need to plan for a four-month voyage to New Zealand. Your bag contains your clothes and other items for the sea voyage. Your trunk contains the rest of your clothes and other items. It is stored away during the voyage.

4 Research: Find a picture of the painting called Embarking for Home by E. Noyce and work out what is happening in it.

ISBN 9780170182256

A Voyage of Luck

Focus
- Events have causes and effects.
- People respond to challenges as individuals and groups.
- People move between places which has results for people and places.
- Ideas and actions of people in the past helped shape society.

- The voyage usually took four to six months. In bad weather, it might take longer.
- The voyage was across a huge expanse of ocean. Immigrants had no idea of what awaited them. Friends and relatives who went to the dock to see them off thought that if the immigrants survived the voyage, they might be killed or die once they got ashore in New Zealand.
- Cabin passengers, who paid their own fares, were on the after-deck. They had to provide their own furnishings such as beds. They might include items like pianos.
- Steerage passengers were assisted immigrants. They were under the main deck. There was no room for them to bring furniture.
- Live animals on board provided food and milk. Poultry might be kept in cages on the poop. Cows, goats, sheep and pigs would be housed below decks.
- Possible problems during voyages included leaks, gales breaking masts and ripping sails, waves washing through hatches, crews becoming violent, greasy decks causing accidents, cramped conditions spreading disease, food and water becoming bad.

- Because of the poor and unsafe lights, there was always a danger of fire. In 1874 the *Cospatrick* was on a voyage from England to New Zealand with immigrants on board. Fire broke out south of the Cape of Good Hope. Only three of 471 people survived.
- Sea-sickness was a constant worry. Many people died from it.
- Many immigrants lost their lives on the ship before they reached New Zealand. If a ship was becalmed and fresh water and supplies ran out, small children died first. On one immigrant ship in 1842, 65 children died.
- Boredom was a big problem. One thing that kept immigrants hopeful and entertained was searching the horizon for land.

START

1 Arrive at ship. Stores, ropes, boxes cover decks. Rain causes mud. -2

2 200 people in steerage causes over-crowding. Only a few candles. -3

3 Ship sets sail. Many passengers immediate sea-sick.

-3 Water on b has gone It smells All pray rain.

+1 A little rain but then becalmed in tropics. Very hot.

24

+5 Some men tie ropes around middles, crew lower them overboard.

25

+2 Sharks sighted. Another ship passes. Captains talk through trumpets.

26

27

+4 Heavy rain. Passengers use pots and pans to catch water.

28

Doctor issues each child a teaspoon of treacle and sulphur. +2

29

Riot in steerage. Crew throw buckets of water over people fighting. -3

ISBN 9780170182256

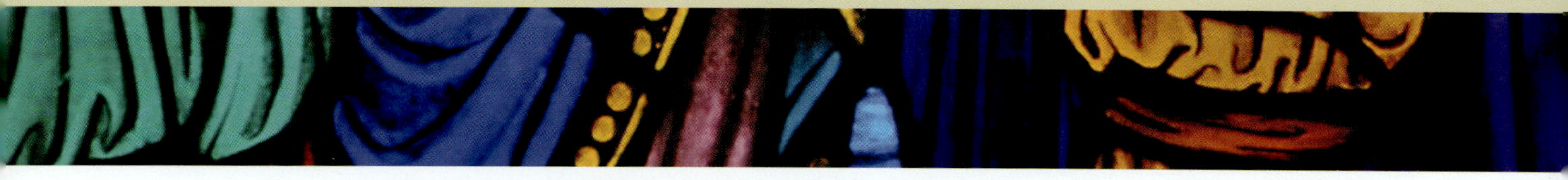

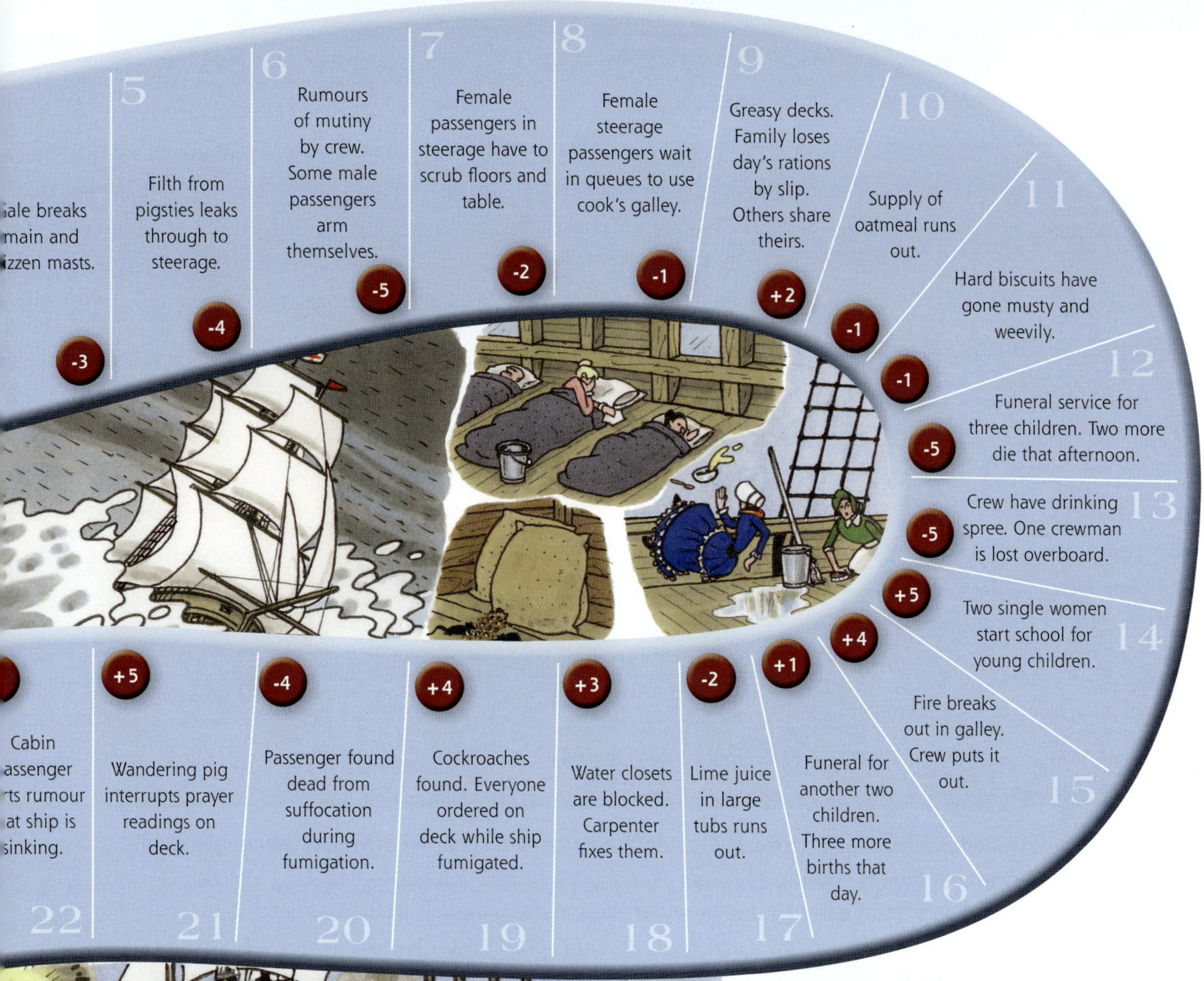

...ale breaks
...main and
...zzen masts.
-3

5
Filth from pigsties leaks through to steerage.
-4

6
Rumours of mutiny by crew. Some male passengers arm themselves.
-5

7
Female passengers in steerage have to scrub floors and table.
-2

8
Female steerage passengers wait in queues to use cook's galley.
-1

9
Greasy decks. Family loses day's rations by slip. Others share theirs.
+2

10
Supply of oatmeal runs out.
-1

11
Hard biscuits have gone musty and weevily.
-1

12
Funeral service for three children. Two more die that afternoon.
-5

13
Crew have drinking spree. One crewman is lost overboard.
-5

14
Two single women start school for young children.
+5

15
Fire breaks out in galley. Crew puts it out.
+4

16
Funeral for another two children. Three more births that day.
+1

17
Lime juice in large tubs runs out.
-2

18
Water closets are blocked. Carpenter fixes them.
+3

19
Cockroaches found. Everyone ordered on deck while ship fumigated.
+4

20
Passenger found dead from suffocation during fumigation.
-4

21
Wandering pig interrupts prayer readings on deck.
+5

22
Cabin
...assenger
...rts rumour
...at ship is
...sinking.

...0
...mate's
...nday. All
...nigrants
...ed with
...rog.
+4

31
Another four deaths and three births. A woman dies in childbirth.
-3

32
A sailor kills a porpoise with a harpoon.
+3

33
Land is sighted.
+5

FINISH

Activities

1. Play A Voyage of Luck. Use a coin for moves. Heads = 3 spaces, tails = 2 spaces. Make a note of the numbers you land on. Go to the finish. Then swap your set of numbers with your partner. This is part of the luck. Total your score. If it is a plus number you had a very lucky voyage. The highest score wins.
2. As an immigrant describe your voyage to New Zealand. Include a description of the ship and your diet.
3. Research: Find out what was happening in Ireland in the late 1840s that made many people immigrate.

ISBN 9780170182256

Change in Housing

Focus
- Events have causes and effects.
- People move between places which has results for people and places.

Once immigrants landed in New Zealand they were settlers. Immigration changed their lives, although not always in expected ways. One change was housing.

Like the Polynesian settlers, most early European settlers had to use materials in the new land to make houses and furniture. A house might be four poles stuck in the ground with fern on top. It might be a cave, a hollow tree-trunk, a tent on the beach.

Because there were few cabinet-makers for quite a while, settlers made their own furniture. Whalers, for example, used joints from a whale's backbone as stools.

Bricks and stones were common building materials in Britain. Bricks in New Zealand were mostly imported. Usually they were ballast – material used to stabilise the ship that carried immigrants. Settlers saved bricks for special things like chimneys. Some settlers made mud bricks and dried them in the sun.

An early type of hut was the V hut. It was small and settlers could build it in a day. Its wooden walls met at the top. At one end was a door. Bunks lined each side. The kitchen was a fire outside.

A few wealthy immigrants brought out pre-cut wooden cottages.

In the north, the raupo whare was the most common house. Settlers used vines to tie raupo to posts and rafters. They thatched the roof with rushes and tussock. Even if they used imported windows and doors, the whare was still very cheap to build.

In the south, settlers needed stronger houses to cope with the climate. Some built huts of earth sods. The most common hut was the slab (timber), cob (clay) and ricker (sapling) hut, usually called a cob house.

Building your cob house

How to make cob

Find a supply of clay. Dig a circular ditch. Tether a pack-horse in the middle of the ditch. Feed clay into the ditch. Move the horse around and keep adding chopped tussock and water into the ditch until they are puddled to the right mixture.

ISBN 9780170182256

Rooms in your house

- kitchen and living room with fireplace
- main bedroom
- guest chamber (second bedroom; space at one end for stores and tools, bunks for children at other end)
- annexe (lean-to) for bathroom

Your tools

- axe
- adze (like an axe but blade long and skinny with a curve in it)
- hammer
- maul (heavy hammer for splitting wood)
- crowbar
- ewbanks (hand-forged nails)
- saw
- shovel
- wedges (objects pushed between things to separate them)
- plumb bob (lead weight attached to string)

Your building materials

- black pine (matai) for uprights
- black birch (beech) for slabs
- imported bricks for chimney
- cob for filling

Your furniture

- crockery
- arm-chair
- 4 pictures
- 3 flax mats
- round copper (big vessel for boiling clothes to wash them)
- apple crusher
- foot-propelled bellows
- iron kettle
- pots & billies
- candles
- imported dresser
- flour barrel
- 3 packing cases
- 2 camp ovens
- teak sea-chest
- tin bath
- brass-inlaid clock
- 2 red twill curtains
- dressing table (calico round a box)
- bed (made of saplings)
- mattresses (filled with bracken)
- tin oil lamp

Activities

1 Draw and label a V hut and a raupo whare.

2 The box to the right contains steps in building your cob house. They are in the wrong order. Rearrange them into the right order.

3 Describe how easy or hard it would be to build this house.

4 Draw a cross-section of a wall and label each building material.

5 Draw a floor plan showing each room. Show where each piece of furniture goes.

6 Not one modern service is available to you in your cob hut. Draw a chart and fill it out.

Modern service	How I will cope without this
electricity	

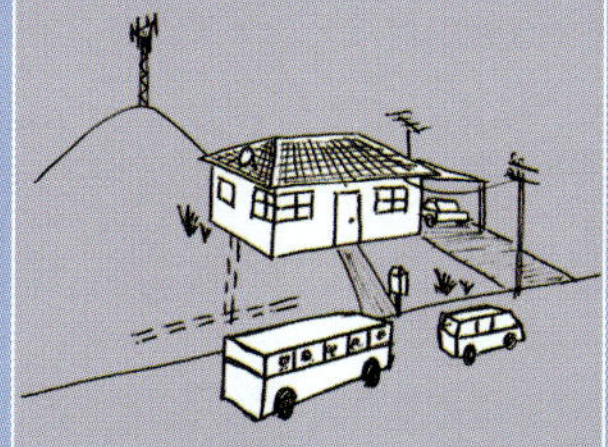

7 Research: Find illustrations of early Tauiwi housing in New Zealand.

Thatch with layers of snow grass. Sow layers on with big needle.
Line up uprights and saw off level.
Start to build inner walls by nailing rickers horizontally on inner faces of uprights. Begin at ground level. Walls will be two feet (2/3m) thick.
Sketch plan on ground.
Split slabs to make vertical weatherboards. Dig in at bottom, nail to plates at top.
Choose site. Consider wind, firewood, water.
Spike top plates down to uprights.
Build roof frame of saplings for rafters. Adze level. Nail at 8 inches (23cms) apart with small saplings in between.
Pack in layers of cob between slabs and rickers.
Sink corner posts, intermediates and door opening. Plumb and ram in tightly.
Level clay floor by light watering and sweep.
Build fireplace and chimney.

ISBN 9780170182256

7

Finding a Job

Focus

- Events have causes and effects.
- People respond to challenges as individuals and groups.
- People move between places which has results for people and places.
- Ideas and actions of people in the past helped shape society.
- Economic decisions have an impact on people and communities.

Immigrants who went to New Zealand Company settlements needed to find jobs. Here are some job descriptions and early tools of ten important craftsmen.

Craftsmen

carpenter	**saddler**
bootmaker	**stone dresser**
cooper	**farm labourer**
shipwright	**sailmaker**
wheelwright	**blacksmith**

Job Descriptions

1. Uses hand bellows to heat a furnace and stand for shoeing. Also makes tools for other craftsmen.
2. Has to make heavy, hard-wearing products as those brought by settlers are useless in the roadless, bush-covered new country. Uses knives, iron feet and holders, needles and hammers.
3. Is never short of work because there is a big demand for his services and products. Uses a pit saw and gets to know kauri logs well.
4. Makes his product by fitting staves (narrow strips of wood or iron) into iron hoops. Has to shave staves and must be accurate. Uses long jointer and raised blade.
5. May have plough but it will be useless until stumps are cleared. Uses rake, scythe and sickle. Makes other tools as needed.
6. Makes equipment for a recently-introduced form of transport. Uses cutting tools, stitch wheels, awl (punches holes in leather) and hammers.
7. Works with canvas. Has to protect his hand with leather strap with hole for thumb. This is reinforced with small iron plate. Uses knives and needles.
8. Product is vital for trading country. Works with wood around harbour or port.
9. Uses a mill bill to cut, sharpen and repair grinding edges of big round objects used to grind wheat in mills.
10. Makes products from timber. Uses an axe to cut the timber, then an adze and spokeshave (tool with handle on each side of blade) to make the rounded shape.

ISBN 9780170182256

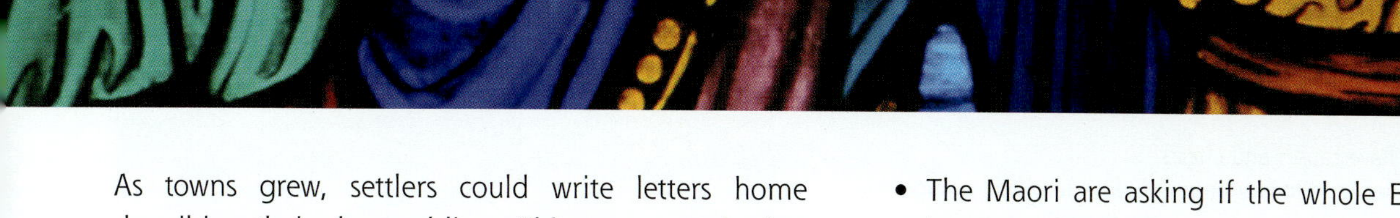

As towns grew, settlers could write letters home describing their changed lives. This encouraged other immigrants to come out. This is called chain immigration. Here are some things settlers put in letters.

- Although many children died on ships coming out, children here have a healthy life. Working class children are allowed to go barefooted. They play their English games of hop-scotch, blind man's buff, oranges and lemons, hunt the slipper, and so on. However, they spend much time outside. There are no schools yet except for a private one for wealthy settlers' children.
- Bartering with the Maori has been a cheap way to live. I swapped three old shirts for a kit of potatoes, and two big spoonfuls of sugar for a pig.
- We have a police magistrate, some shops, hospital and the start of some roads. There is no workhouse for the poor – they are looked after by their families.

Until 1967 New Zealand did not have decimal currency. It had pounds, shillings and pence.

one pound ($2)	=	£1
	=	20 shillings (20/-)
1 shilling (1/-)	=	12 pence
	=	12d
one shilling and sixpence	=	1/6

Until 1969 New Zealand did not have the metric system. It had pounds and quarts.

1 pound	=	1 lb
	=	0.45kg
1 quart	=	1 qt
	=	0.946 litres

Activities

1 Match the craftsmen to the job descriptions.

2 Andrew is 23-years-old. His father in England has sent Andrew to New Zealand with a few pounds in cash and instructions to make something of himself. Andrew decides to go into business. On the right are important events in Andrew's life. Put them in the right order to show how Andrew set about obeying his father.

3 Discuss which of the ten craftsmen Andrew would need.

4 Write a letter home for Andrew. His brother in England has a wife and six children. He wants to know whether he should immigrate. Put some advice to him in the letter.

5 Explain a use for each of these items: spokeshave, mill bill, awl, stave, sickle, furnace, bullock dray, schooner.

6 Research: Find an account by or about an early immigrant to New Zealand.

- The Maori are asking if the whole European tribe has come here to live because so many immigrants arrive.
- In 1842, a big fire along the waterfront burnt all the houses. There have also been some frightening earthquakes.
- The average daily wage is 6-8 shillings.
- Some prices are:
  - milk (qt) = 4d
  - beef (1 lb) = 8d
  - butter (1 lb) = 1/3
  - tea (1 lb) = 2/0
  - cheese (1 lb) = 1/0
  - mutton (1 lb) = 8d
  - bread (1 lb) = 4d
  - sugar (1 lb) = 5d

The events of Andrew's life

- He receives the site of his town section.
- He has made enough money to build a wooden hotel.
- He sets up his own flour mill.
- He buys his own schooner to take the wheat out to the export ship.
- He buys a bullock dray to take wheat out to the schooner.
- He is now a wealthy businessman. He marries and builds a big home.
- The stable is a success. He buys 20 acres of land outside town to grow wheat.
- He sets up his first hotel by putting a barrel of beer in a rough raupo hut on the beach.
- Horses and cattle are being brought in from Australia. He decides to build a stable with profits from his hotel.

ISBN 9780170182256

The Land Gave Them Sheep Runs

Focus

- Events have causes and effects.
- People respond to challenges as individuals and groups.
- People move between places which has results for people and places.
- Exploration creates chances and challenges.
- Ideas and actions of people in the past helped shape society.
- Economic decisions have an impact on people and communities.
- The way people manage resources has an impact on the environment.

The settlers had to be able to make changes to their lifestyles. This was because Wakefield's ideas of tidy, organised English villages surrounded by small mixed farms could not work in the new land.

The diagram shows the main reasons for this.

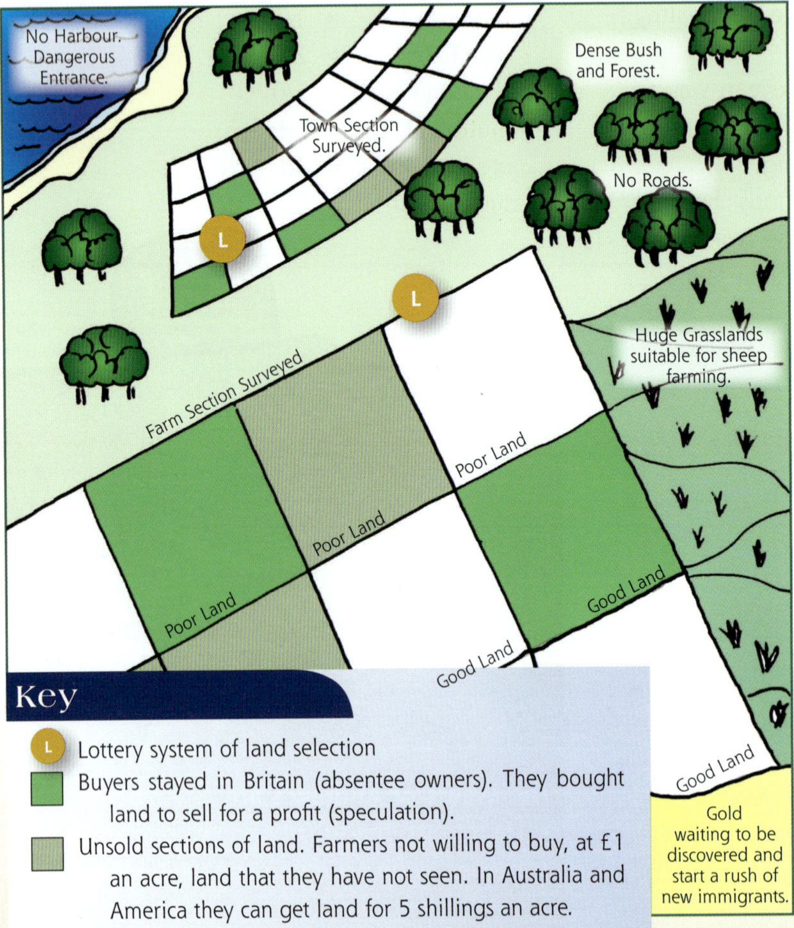

Key

- L — Lottery system of land selection
- Buyers stayed in Britain (absentee owners). They bought land to sell for a profit (speculation).
- Unsold sections of land. Farmers not willing to buy, at £1 an acre, land that they have not seen. In Australia and America they can get land for 5 shillings an acre.

Some immigrants who came to New Zealand with money for the English style mixed farm took one look at their land and decided to go sheep farming instead.They had to be willing to take risks and live in changed conditions until their runs were set up. This was different to how Wakefield had planned the immigrant settlements.

John arrived from London in 1850. He spent a few days looking at land around the new town. He decided to go further into the country and try sheep farming.

'John's Risks' (on page 19) show how he set up his run.

Activities

Look at the information on page 19 before you answer these questions.

1 Describe how a lottery works. Decide if this is the fairest way of allotting sections of land.

2 Explain why Wakefield's ideas did not work.

3 Many of John's actions involved a risk. Match the 9 risks to 9 of John's actions and explain if his action was a high risk or a low risk.

4 List the people with whom John did business.

5 Discuss reasons for these facts about John:

a) He does not marry until he is 35.

b) He will make sure his sons have a good education.

c) He will become important in local and national politics.

d) He prefers not to eat mutton.

e) He would not have survived economically if he had not taken risks.

6 Describe how John changed his environment.

7 Research: Find out what it meant to be the black sheep of a family which exiled you to New Zealand with something called a remittance.

ISBN 9780170182256

John's Risk

Possible risk factors:

- Roof of a hut is always the weak point.
- Maximum pace of sheep and bullock dray is 2 mph (3.2 kph).
- No wire fences until the 1860s and no swing gates until the late 1850s.
- Rivers are always liable to flood.
- Fire is always liable to go out of control.
- Other people may not be trustworthy.
- No proper land surveys.
- Nearest neighbour is 100km away, nearest town is 112km away.
- Scab, disease which attacks sheep, is easily spread from one flock to another.

John arrives in New Zealand with £3,000. He is 26-years-old. He is the youngest son of an upper class family. Although he has had a good education, he has had no training for work.

1 John leases land from Maori for £12 a year.

2 He pays £1 each for 1,000 ewes. They arrive in port on a ship from Australia.

3 He hires a shepherd for £60 a year.

4 He hires an agent in town to send out stores to his run and arrange for wool to be shipped to England.

5 John and his shepherd take the sheep to the run. They have a pack-horse each loaded with stores. There are three rivers to cross.

6 John hires Maori to build a raupo whare and huts along boundaries.

7 John and his shepherd live on tea and damper. They barter some with Maori for potatoes and cabbage.

8 A gale takes the whare's roof. Next day the whole whare collapses.

9 The agent has not sent provisions. The two men are nearly starving. John returns to town. He buys a bullock team. He pays £64 for the dray and £180 for eight bullocks. He loads one and half tons on the dray.

10 John and the shepherd set fire to some tussock to sow clover seed. The hut burns down.

11 At culling time when the old and weak sheep are killed, the men live on mutton.

12 John works all day in wet clothes. He is then ill for two weeks.

13 Part of the next runholder's flock strays on to John's land. John is grazing his sheep close to the boundary.

14 John takes his first wool sacks on the dray to meet the ship. A whaleboat meets the dray in the surf.

By 1859 John is married. He has doubled his money and built a four-roomed house, woolshed, stables, men's quarters. He employs a full-time overseer, bullock driver, two shepherds, two roustabouts. He gives seasonal work to musterers and shearers.

ISBN 9780170182256

The Land Gave Them Gold

Focus

- Events have causes and effects.
- People respond to challenges as individuals and groups.
- People move between places which has results for people and places.
- Exploration creates chances and challenges.
- Ideas and actions of people in the past helped shape society.
- Economic decisions have an impact on people and communities.
- The way people manage resources has an impact on the environment.

By 1850 Wakefield's immigrant schemes had finished. Soon, however, gold was found. This brought a rush of more immigrants from all around the world. They also had to be willing to risk their lives. Always there was the danger of drowning, starving or freezing to death, either on the goldfields or on the way there.

Gold-diggers could be recognised by their clothes and gear.

The gold-digger

ISBN 9780170182256

Some methods for getting the gold

Panning: Put shingle and sand into tin dish. Fill with water. Swirl around until dirt is washed away and gold grains sit at the bottom.

Bore: Pay the runholder £5 for permission to sink bore. Use pick and shovel to make the bore. Lift earth out by buckets on a rope. Wash out in the usual way.

Underground mines: Dig mines and timber entrances for safety. Go down shaft to chop out rocks. Pulley hauls these to surface. Crush rock and treat it with cyanide to get gold.

Cradle: This is shaped like a child's cradle and is about the same size with one end open. The other end has a box with a sieve in it. Sacking covers the bottom. Shovel earth onto the sieve. Ladle water in with a dipper. Keep the cradle rocking. Earth washes out the end and leaves gold caught at the bottom.

Wheelbarrows: Use on beaches. Dig sand at low tide and carry it above high tide mark. Wash it out later.

Riffle (sluice) boxes: Nicknamed Long Toms. Long wooden boxes built as series of terrace-like steps. Wash earth and gravel over these. Lip of each step traps gold and washes away earth. Wash gravel and gold in pan.

Horse whim: Sink shaft. Harness horse to whim (barrel) and walk it in circle to bring earth and gravel up from shaft. Wash out in usual way.

Sluicing: Dig tunnel to divert water from stream or wooden race built to bring water to gold. Water goes through pipes leading to hoses. Hoses spray water at gravel faces or hill to wash gravels through sluice boxes. Hoses are so strong they can kill diggers.

Dredges: Use on river beds and deep wet ground. Work spoon-dredge by hand in shallow, calm water. River current drives wheel-dredge and chain of buckets dig up shingle to pass it through sluice box.

Activities

1. Make a sketch of a digger. Show clothes and gear. Give him or her a nickname. The digger will carry accomodation on his or her back. Add this to your sketch.
2. The digger will be going to Coromandel, or Thames, or Hokitika, or Nelson or Otago. Imagine the digger is starting out from your town. Put arrows to show in which direction the digger will head for each location and write the location by the arrow.
3. If the digger is lucky enough to find gold, he or she will have to carry this in the form of gold dust or nuggets until a bank is reached. Decide where the digger will carry the gold and show this on your sketch.
4. Explain how the gold-digger is helping to change the environment.
5. The gold-digger cannot compete with a company that has heavy machinery and equipment to build fancy water races and so on. Sort out which methods the individual gold-digger would use to get gold and which methods the big companies would use.
6. Research: Find at least three pieces of information you could use in an assignment about early gold-diggers.

ISBN 9780170182256

Changing Family Fortunes

Focus

- Events have causes and effects.
- People respond to challenges as individuals and groups.
- People move between places which has results for people and places.
- Exploration creates chances and challenges.
- Ideas and actions of people in the past helped shape society.
- Economic decisions have an impact on people and communities.
- The way people manage resources has an impact on the environment.

- Gabriel Reed of Australia discovered gold in 1861 at what became Gabriel's Gully. The gold rush increased the population of Otago from less than 13,000 to 30,000.
- By 1863 gold accounted for more than 70% of the value of New Zealand's exports. It continued to exceed 10% until well into the 20th century.
- It is estimated that over the 100 years from 1860, over 750 tonnes of gold was exported from New Zealand.

It is 1861. James, his wife and their four children, live in a tiny town. He owns the general store. His 18-year-old brother William works for him. News of a gold strike nearby races through town. William is excited. James, however, wants him to stay and help with the business. Already people are rushing into the area. The word is that the strike is huge. James knows that thousands of people will arrive. Chart 1 shows some things James finds out about the diggings to try to persuade William not to go. William is unconvinced. James agrees to provide provisions for him from the store.

William is unsuccessful on the goldfields. James becomes wealthy staying in town and sending provisions to the diggings. Chart 2 shows people like James who did well from gold rushes.

Chart 1

The diggings and how to get there

- The shortest route is over the mountains. This is often blocked by snow. If you lose the track, you will die of cold.
- A second route goes around a lake. The road is usually a bog. Loaded drays sink to their axles. Bundles of flax can be laid across for traction.

Types of digging

Heavy digging through clay and gravel to bedrock. The few metres above bedrock has the gold. This is called dirt wash and has to be carried to running water.

Winter on the field

Shelter is a tent. Fuel is for cooking, not warmth. Once the billy has boiled, sticks of wood have to be put out and saved. Boots and clothes freeze overnight and have to be thawed. When a thaw melts ice, water will flood the tent. There is danger of hypothermia, starvation and scurvy (lack of vitamin C which causes symptoms such as loose teeth, bleeding gums, red skin lesions.)

Main amusements

Gambling, boxing, dog-fights, drinking, pig-hunting, reading newspapers.

Earnings

Not more than a quarter of the diggers make £5 a day. The rest average 10 shillings. Some have found no gold.

Newspapers

Otago Witness and *Australasian* are 2/6 a copy.

Claim

The size of each digger's claim is 24 square feet.

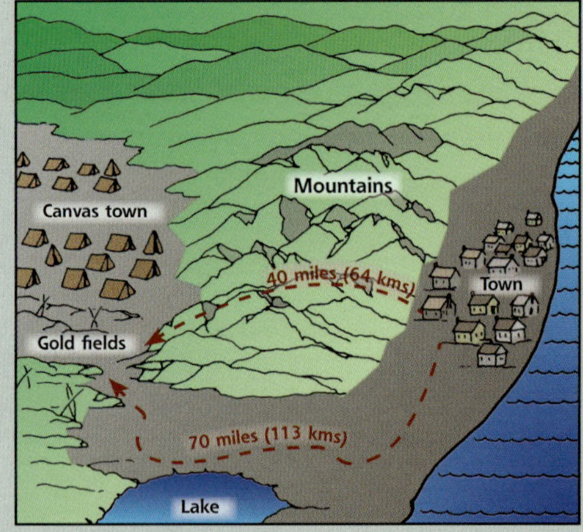

Ratio of females to males

To every 100 males, 1 female.

Prices on the goldfield

sugar	2/6 pound
soap	2/6 pound
bread	7 shillings for 4 lb loaf
potatoes	unavailable
tea	5 shillings pound
flour	2/6 pound
mutton	3 shillings pound
timber	Very scarce and very expensive
an old candle box	£1
an empty guncase	£3
rough pole	£1
load of brushwood	£5

Transport

To get a ton of goods from town to goldfield costs £90.

ISBN 9780170182256

Chart 2

People who did well from the gold rush:

- shipping clerk
- ship owner
- shipping manager
- undertaker
- hotel keeper
- casino owner
- clergyman
- sawyer
- carter
- warden (policeman on diggings; his wife is used as warden for females)
- mounted policeman (escorts gold from diggings)
- store-keeper
- bushranger (ambushes gold on way back to town)
- gold-receiver (issues mining digging rights, makes sure gold gets to bank)
- woman running boarding-house
- barman
- theatre owner
- surveyor
- butcher
- carpenter
- banker
- road-builder
- bullock-driver
- dancing-girl
- baker
- barber
- tent-maker
- stage coach driver
- stonemason
- blacksmith
- workshop-engineer.

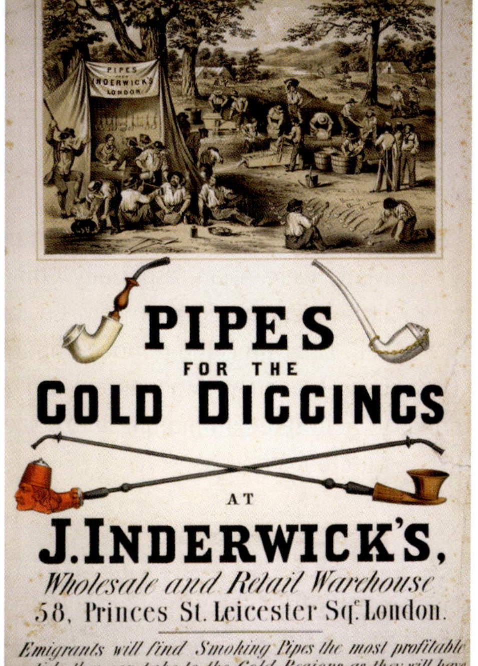

Activities

1 Give ten arguments that James uses to try to persuade William not to go to the diggings.

2 List things William takes to the diggings. He is walking so he has to carry it all.

3 Copy the map. Check out the list of people who did well from the gold rush. Put the name of each person on your map where you think he or she belongs. Where a person is on the move, put him or her along a track. For example, there would be a hotel in the new canvas town near the goldfield and one in the old town.

4 The box contains an extract from *The Otago Witness*. Explain what it suggests about how gold rushes changed the environment.

5 Research: Find some statistics that show how important gold was to the 19th century economy.

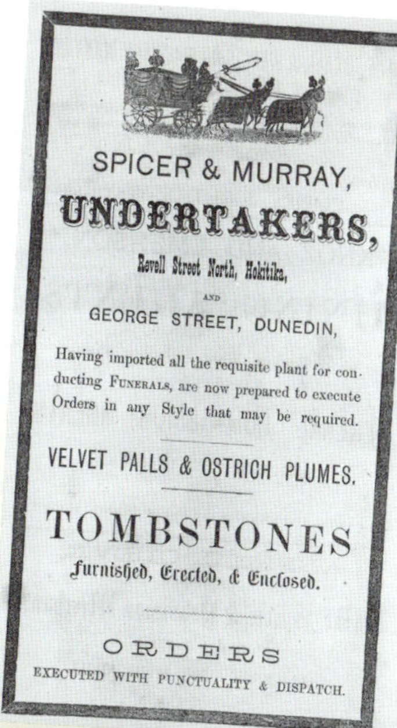

The Otago Witness

The town (Dunedin) is half tents, whole colonies of them being inhabited by women and children whose husbands and fathers are up at the diggings … Mud houses are to be seen …. I noticed one domicile the other day built entirely of tin biscuit boxes battered out.

But They're Different To Us

FOCUS

- Events have causes and effects.
- People respond to challenges as individuals and groups.
- People move between places which has results for people and places.
- Exploration creates chances and challenges.
- Cultural interaction impacts on cultures and societies.
- Ideas and actions of people in the past helped shape society.
- Economic decisions have an impact on people and communities.
- The way people manage resources has an impact on the environment.

Gold rushes brought the first big numbers of non-British immigrants. Many were Asian, especially Chinese. Indians tended to arrive a little later. Immigrants from Ceylon (today Sri Lanka) came later still. Later on came refugee immigrants from places like Vietnam, Laos, Myanmar, Afghanistan. Today there are special organisations to help settle immigrants into society. In the 19th century it was a different story.

Discrimination
to treat people of different religion, race or culture differently to how you treat other people

Prejudice
feelings, usually of dislike, towards a race or group of people and not wanting to change your feelings about them

British settlers saw the Chinese as different

They wear their hair in long pigtails. They wear coolie hats.	They look different to us.	They make new handles for picks and shovels out of manuka sticks.	They hold Chinese festivals and travel miles to take part in them.
They live in caves, grass sod huts, mud and stone huts.	They make lanterns for tunnels and shafts out of candles with wire handles.	They smoke opium pipes. They work seven days a week.	They grow their own vegetables in gardens along river banks.
They patch moleskin trousers thrown away by other diggers.	They like gambling better than drinking alcohol.	They keep to themselves in small groups.	They speak their own language or very poor English.
Their religion is a mix of Eastern beliefs such as Confucianism and Buddhism.	They use sacking as raincoats.	They eat mostly rice and some imported Chinese foods.	They eat eels they get out of the streams.
They're everywhere; there are many Chinaman's Hills and Chinaman's Creeks.	They work long hours – 10 to 12 hours a day.	They are inhumanly patient with their sieving and resieving.	They make their wheelbarrows out of old boxes.
They follow us. They set themselves up on claims that we say are finished.	They work through tailings (left-over rock and earth from mines).	They use up tailings which we might need to fall back on in tough times.	They carry belongings on bamboo shoulder poles.
They come here without wives which means they'll chase British girls.	They ship their dead back to China.	They don't intend staying here to contribute; they aim to return to China.	They send their money out of the country to China.

ISBN 9780170182256

This is you ...

(1880 male or female)

- You come from England. You believe New Zealand should be made as English as possible.
- You observe Sunday as a day of rest. You go to a Church of England service whenever you can.
- You believe that men should look like males and women should look like females.
- You have a brother who makes a living by carrying food to the goldfields.
- You and your spouse own a store. You sell tools, tents, digging tools and clothes to gold-diggers.
- Your cousin works for a company. He and some friends are discussing ways of getting better working conditions.

In 1871 you and your gold-digging mates in Central Otago ask Parliament to stop letting the Chinese into New Zealand. 'Otherwise,' you say, 'there will be bloodshed.'

A special committee gives you its answer. The Chinese are industrious, frugal, orderly, not likely to introduce infectious diseases, and no special risk to morality. There are not sufficient grounds to stop them coming here.

However, in 1881, official discrimination against the Chinese begins. In that year Chinese numbers peaked at just over 5,000. This was about 40 percent of Otago's gold-diggers. By then, some Chinese had shifted to goldfields on the West Coast. Others were working as shopkeepers, market-gardeners, shearers and cooks.

Activities

1 Explain the meanings of prejudice, discrimination, opium, special committee, frugal, orderly, morality.

2 Make up two Prejudice Assessment charts and fill in details. In the first one you are British or Maori. In the second one, you are Chinese. Both are for the year 1880.

3 In 2002 the New Zealand Prime Minister apologised to the Chinese for the discimination laws and tax imposed on Chinese immigrants. Explain how this shows attitudes of society change.

4 Research: Choie Sew Hoy developed a new type of bucket dredge to work his Big Beach claim on the Shotover River. This was the beginning for what became known as the New Zealand gold dredge. Find out about this dredge.

Prejudice Assessment:

Name

The Chinese diggers annoy people because:

People	Reason
me	
my brother	
my friends	

We threatened bloodshed because

My opinion of the special committee is

What should be done about the Chinese is

I am / am not prejudiced because

Prejudice Assessment:

The British / Maori annoy me because

In this country I feel

My short-term plans are

My long-term plans are

I am / am not prejudiced because

ISBN 9780170182256

Looking at Cartoons

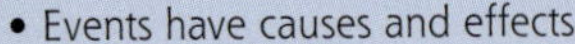

Focus

- Events have causes and effects.
- People move between places which has results for people and places.
- Exploration creates chances and challenges.
- Cultural interaction impacts on cultures and societies.
- Ideas and actions of people in the past helped shape society.

Cartoons show what people thought of events at a particular time. The cartoons here, for example, show what many people in New Zealand thought of Asian immigration.

When you are trying to understand a cartoon, it is useful to try to answer questions about it. For example:

- What date was it drawn?
- Who is the cartoonist?
- Does it have a title?
- Does it have an explanation underneath?
- What is the setting? The environment?
- Are there people in it?
- Do you recognise any of the people?
- What are the people doing?
- Is there speech?
- How do the people look — happy, unhappy?
- What are the people wearing?
- Can you tell what the cartoonist thinks about the situation?

Imperial	from the British Empire
Imperial Conference	meeting of leaders of British Empire
poll	head
burden	load, cargo
legislation	laws passed by Government
returned servicemen	people in armed forces back from war
White New Zealand League	group set up to stop Chinese and Indian immigration; known as the White NZ policy
Hindoo	Hindu, person who follows beliefs of Hinduism in India
opium	narcotic from opium poppy

1920
Ellis
Free Lance

Will it come to this!

1920
Blomfield
Observer

1917
Glover
Truth

THE HINDOO PERIL

SHALL POLITICIANS OPE' THE DOOR?

 ISBN 9780170182256

D
1905
Blomfield
Free Lance

Still they come!

E
1920
Ellis
Free Lance

The alien wave!

Discrimination and Prejudice

Restrictions begin with a poll tax - £10 on each Chinese coming into New Zealand. Their numbers are limited in any ship to one Chinese for every 10 tons burden.

1 The poll tax is raised to £100 for each Chinese. This is not removed until 1944.

An Opium Act says police can search without a warrant.

Chinese immigrants must be able to read 100 words of English.

Resident Chinese have to be thumb-printed before they leave New Zealand if they want to be allowed back in.

Although the White New Zealand League is not formed until 1926, many politicians and members of the public believe in a White New Zealand policy and want to stop all Asians coming as immigrants.

2 At an Imperial Conference in 1917, New Zealand is asked to let wives and children of Indian immigrants in New Zealand come as immigrants.

3 Some people are worried that Asians will marry European girls and their children will have problems fitting in to society.

4 After World War 1, more Asian immigrants come. Some work as labourers, others open fruit shops and laundries, others move into market-gardening. Many European market-gardeners say they are threatened by unfair competition.

5 Workers and returned servicemen are also worried they may lose their jobs.

In the early 1930s a bad depression makes many people complain about Asian immigrants. But as economic conditions improve, most people lose their prejudice and stop asking for laws to discriminate against Asians.

Activities

1 Match numbers 1 to 5 on the Discrimination and Prejudice chart with the cartoons to which they refer.
2 Choose two of the cartoons and discuss them.
3 Explain the link between discimination and prejudice, and the White New Zealand policy and League.
4 Research: Find an anti-racist cartoon from any country. For example, there is a great Dr Suess one.

ISBN 9780170182256

The Land Gave Them Kauri Gum

Focus

- Events have causes and effects.
- People move between places which has results for people and places.
- Ideas and actions of people in the past helped shape society.
- Economic decisions have an impact on people and communities.
- The way people manage resources has an impact on the environment.
- People make decisions about access to and use of resources.

Data on kauri gum industry

Boom time	1875-1925
Location	Gumfields scattered from Coromandel Peninsula and lower Waikato to way up in north of North Island.
Numbers	Thousands of diggers. Some had wives and children with them.
Who	Many different peoples such as Russians, Finns, Dalmatians, English.
Types	Some diggers were aristocrats (upper class). Some were ex-prisoners from Mount Eden jail who had been given a railway ticket to gumfields. Many were settlers struggling to make farms. During winter and in economic depressions they went gum-digging to earn money.
Uses of gum	Exported to be used in making of varnish and linoleum. Gum industry declined when synthetics (man-made) were used instead.
Where gum came from	Fossil gum was dug from the ground. It had a thin film of red brown rust. Diggers had to scrape it off with a knife. It was a slow and boring job done at night. Tree gum came from a live tree. As the first branch of a kauri tree was many metres up, this was dangerous. Diggers sometimes made cuts in a tree to bleed gum out. This could be punished with a fine or imprisonment.
Types of gumfields	Private land had to be leased. Or the owner might instead become a storekeeper. He bought gum from diggers and supplied them with goods. He might give 'grub stakes' to a new chum. This was a supply of gear and tucker (food) on credit. Crown land was open freely to all diggers.
Best gum	Hard and bright.
Worst gum	Soft, black, chalky.
Averages	A full sack weighed 11/4cwt (63 kg). Well-scraped, good quality gum got 4d to 5d a pound (about 9c per kg).
Methods for getting gum	Paddocking (light digging over the surface), deep digging, using a gum spear to find gum and a hook to bring it to the surface, draining a swamp, using water races to sluice mud from an area.

 ISBN 9780170182256

Digger's house

This is a tent or raupo whare or sacks spread over stakes. Cooking is done outside. Seats and cupboards are empty boxes. The table is old boards on teatree stakes.

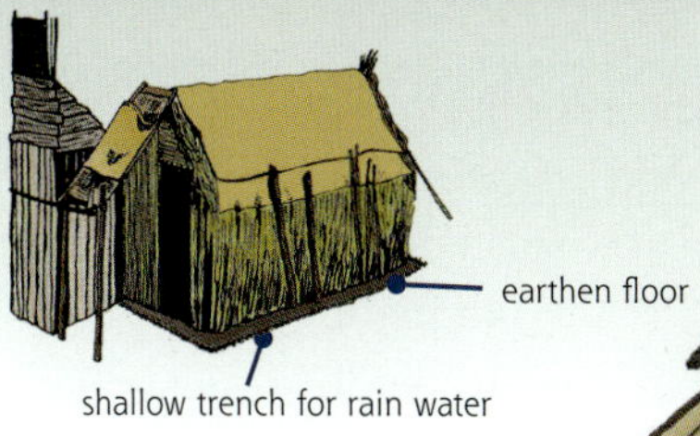

earthen floor

shallow trench for rain water

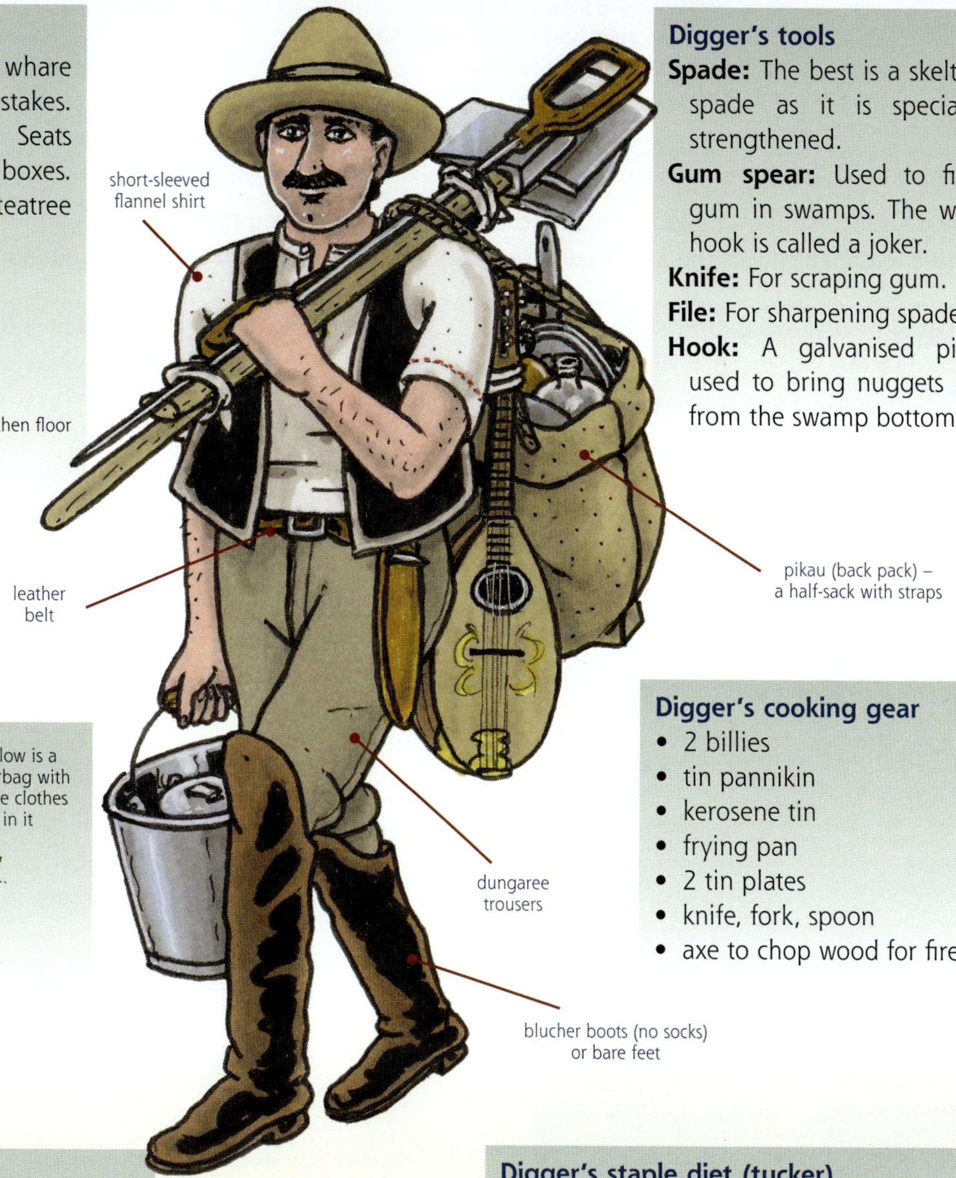

short-sleeved flannel shirt

leather belt

Digger's tools

Spade: The best is a skelton spade as it is specially strengthened.

Gum spear: Used to find gum in swamps. The wire hook is called a joker.

Knife: For scraping gum.

File: For sharpening spade.

Hook: A galvanised pipe used to bring nuggets up from the swamp bottom.

pikau (back pack) – a half-sack with straps

Digger's bed

sacking

pillow is a flourbag with spare clothes in it

teatree poles supported by forked teatree stakes

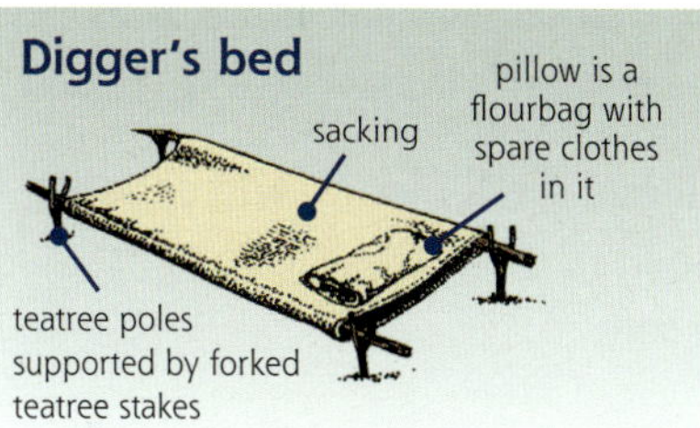

Digger's cooking gear

- 2 billies
- tin pannikin
- kerosene tin
- frying pan
- 2 tin plates
- knife, fork, spoon
- axe to chop wood for fire

dungaree trousers

blucher boots (no socks) or bare feet

Sundays

- play pitch and toss (coin game), crown and anchor (dice game), poker dice
- sleeps
- has a bath in a creek
- scrapes gum
- carves gum
- washes and mends clothes

Digger's staple diet (tucker)

Main foods are bread, butter, hard biscuits, jam, potatoes, tinned meat.The digger takes a billy and tucker to the gumfield in the pikau. He or she leaves the pikau under a teatree and wears a side-bag during the day. At midday the digger boils the billy, puts in tea and sugar, and eats a lunch of bread which has been wrapped in newspaper.

Activities

1 Explain why gum-digging was an extractive industry.

2 Describe the differences between Crown land and private land, and between fossil gum and tree gum, and between paddocking and using a gum spear.

3 Discuss how gum-digging could help families, and help the national economy.

4 Research: Find the names of two books, and two museums (or Gum-digger Parks) that would tell you about gum-digging.

ISBN 9780170182256

You Are a Gum-Digger

Focus

- Events have causes and effects.
- People respond to challenges as individuals and groups.
- People move between places which has results for people and places.
- Cultural interaction impacts on cultures and societies.
- Ideas and actions of people in the past helped shape society.
- Economic decisions have an impact on people and communities.
- The way people manage resources has an impact on the environment.

To be a successful gum-digger, you need to be physically fit. You have to be able to make decisions. You have to have reasonable luck. The actual skills, such as using your gear, will take you about a month to learn.

How to make a digger's lantern

Soak a piece of string in kerosene. Tie it around a quart bottle a few centimetres from the bottom. Light the string and break the bottle at the string line. Trim a candle. Turn the jar upside down. Fit the candle into the neck of the jar.

Some basic expenses

skelton spade	=	5/9d
butter	=	1s per lb
sugar	=	4d per lb
potates	=	1d per lb
jam	=	7d per tin
biscuits	=	4d per lb
tin plate	=	1s
pannikin	=	3d
billy	=	9d

Note: 1 shilling = 12d = 12 pennies = 1/-

Gum carving

Most popular are crosses, anchors, hearts. Polish with emery paper, then with different grades of sandpaper. Gloss with kerosene rag.

How to make chewing gum

Boil fossil gum until plastic. Add enough milk juice from the native thistle to make the gum soft.

Activities

1 Make up your Total Earnings Chart as shown. You will probably need at least two pages for this. Numbers in brackets refer to the maximum possible pieces of gum to be earned. Your marker will give you a mark out of 60 gum pieces and then you can total your earnings.

- Each gum piece weighs 4 pounds. The gum dealer is paying 4d a pound for gum.
- Ratings (in shillings):
  65 and over = excellent,
  40-64 = reasonably secure,
  20-39 = cause for alarm,
  38 and below= struggling for survival.

My Total Earnings Chart
(12 days work)

My name ....

Location of field (1) ....

Type of field (1) ....

List of working gear (5) ....

Reason I am a gum-digger (5) ....

....

How I made:

my whare (8) ....
my bed (3) ....
my pikau (2) ....
my furniture (5) ....
my best gum carving (6) ....
my favourite dessert (4) ....

Sketch of my living and working area (10)

The invention that I am working on to make my job easier (10)

Total gum pieces earned	....
Total weight (pounds)	....
Total in money	....

Minus expenses which are

new Skelton spade =
1 lb butter =
2 lbs sugar =
10 lbs potatoes =
1 tin jam =
5 lbs biscuits =
1 billy =

TOTAL = ...

My total earnings

ISBN 9780170182256

Activities

2 Make your gum-digging decisions. Flip a coin to see what your score is. Heads = plus, tails = minus. Make a note of your decisions and total your score. Then discuss which decisions you made were the right ones and which were the wrong ones.

	Decision		Outcome
1	You decide to try paddocking even though you have been told the area has been picked over before.	+	You collect several sacks of high quality gum.
		–	You find no gum worth keeping and you break your new spade on tangled roots.
2	It is pouring with rain but you decide to keep on working.	+	The rain stops after a few minutes.
		–	You catch a chill and have to rest up for a week.
3	You decide to light a fire to burn off scrub and make digging easier.	+	The fire is kept under control and the burn is good.
		–	You lose control of the fire, burn down a farmer's shed and burn through the peat which damages the gum.
4	You decide to go to town for some relaxation.	+	You spend the evening singing songs from your homeland.
		–	You get into a fight with some British diggers and end up with two black eyes and a sprained wrist.
5	You join a group to drain a big swamp.	+	The swamp is rich and you find a lot of gum.
		–	You find an English digger who didn't help drain the swamp, working on it. You get into a fight with him.
6	You decide to work an undrained area of swamp for a week.	+	You lease the land from the owner and find a lot of gum.
		–	The owner cheats you and you are arrested for trespassing.
7	You decide to try truck – in exchange for working the land you agree to buy your goods from and sell your gum to the owner who sets himself up as a storekeeper.	+	The storekeeper is very fair in all his dealings with you.
		–	The storekeeper charges you very high prices for your goods and pays you very low prices for your gum.
8	Someone has stolen your new gum spear. You decide you know who it is.	+	You avoid a fight by making another spear out of an old spade handle and fence wire.
		–	You make an accusation but it turns out to be wrong and you lose a friend.
9	You decide to move on to another field.	+	The owner of your old field gives you back your credit (the balance of goods bought and gum sold).
		–	The owner refuses to give you back your credit. You have to buy goods you don't need to get your money back.
10	You think the storekeeper is cheating by using fixed scales and charging too much for the weight of the sack containing the gum. You decide to accuse him.	+	The British diggers have found the same and back you up. The storekeeper agrees to use your scales and weigh the sacks properly.
		–	The British diggers and storekeeper won't listen to you and tell you to go back to your own country.

3 Research: Find out why historians say 'Auckland was built on gum'.

Immigrants From Dalmatia

Focus

- Events have causes and effects.
- People move between places which has results for people and places.
- Cultural interaction impacts on cultures and societies.
- Ideas and actions of people in the past helped shape society.
- Economic decisions have an impact on people and communities.
- The way people manage resources has an impact on the environment.
- People make decisions about access to and use of resources.

Dalmatia is a province of Croatia. Croatia is on the peninsula that also has countries such as Serbia, Bosnia and Herzegovina, Montenegro, Albania and Greece. When Dalmatians first came to New Zealand in the 1880s the Austro-Hungarian Empire ruled Dalmatia. This is why people in New Zealand often called Dalmatians Austrians. Later Dalmatia became part of a country called Yugoslavia. This is why Dalmatians were sometimes called Yugoslavs. Later still, Yugoslavia broke up and Dalmatia became part of a new country called Croatia.

By the 1880s there were not enough jobs in Dalmatia. Dalmatians liked to work hard. Many people fished or worked on ships. Dalmatian ship-owners were not doing well. They were slow to change from sail to steam.

Vineyards had done well in Dalmatia. However, a disease called phylloxera attacked plants. It destroyed almost the whole industry.

Dalmatia was over-populated. There was not enough land to farm. New Zealand had a lot of space.

Dalmatia did not have its own government. The people did not always like Austrian laws.

North Auckland's climate was good for Dalmatians. Dalmatia had a Mediterranean climate although there was a chilly north wind called Bora. Winters were mild and rainy. Summers were hot.

The immigrants from Dalmatia were called many names by people in New Zealand. A more polite one was 'Chinese of the North'. Like the Chinese gold-diggers, Dalmatians faced a wall of prejudice.

One law people hated was military conscription. Austrians said Dalmatians had to go and be soldiers. This meant they could be sent from villages to places like Italy.

Most Dalmatians who came to New Zealand went to North Auckland. They went to work as gum-diggers. They did not have to be able to speak good English for that job.

When one or two members of a family or village had got settled in New Zealand, another son or friend would come out to join them.

The Wall of Prejudice

- They dig acre by acre and keep going until they have completely worked the area out.
- They are like a plague of locusts. They will make New Zealand poor.
- They live on the 'smell of an oily rag'.
- They will never speak proper English.
- They used to make and drink wine. This means they are not suitable immigrants at all.
- They will always marry within their own community which is not wise.
- They are incapable of understanding how the English like to work for themselves, not for the good of the whole group.
- They will glut the gum market and force gum prices down.
- They average 31s 6d a week compared to the British 26s a week.
- Having their own newspapers shows they dislike English.
- They work as a team, usually of 20 or more diggers. This makes them intimidating (like bullies).
- They couldn't care less about helping the development of the country.
- They complain there are no Catholic festivals or religious observances here.
- When they have ruined the market, they'll take on labouring jobs and work for less pay so people will hire them instead of British workers.

ISBN 9780170182256

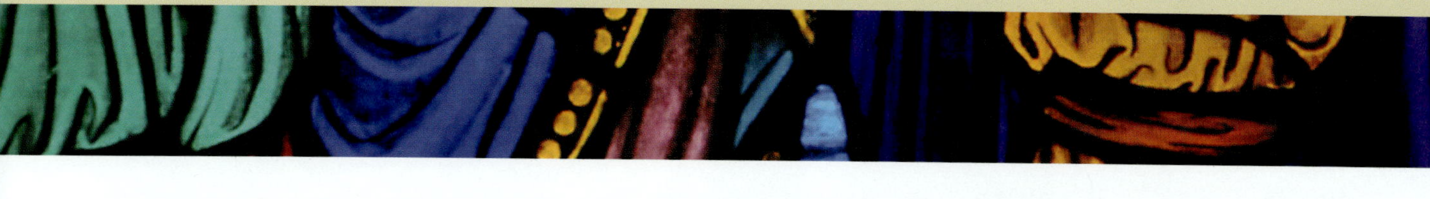

The man in the cartoon is Dick Seddon. He was Prime Minister of New Zealand. He said Dalmatians were like locusts spoiling British settlers' land.

In 1893 and 1898 two special groups called Royal Commissions were set up by Parliament to sort out facts from opinions about Dalmatians. They fired rocks at the wall of prejudice by saying Dalmatians were:

- good at saving money
- hard-working
- good at avoiding debt
- good at problem-solving
- not drunkards
- energetic
- honest
- well-behaved.

The Dalmatian Cartoon

As happened with the Chinese immigrants, however, some politicians and members of the public were not convinced. In 1898, 1908, and 1910 laws were passed which put aside the best gumfields for British, Maori and naturalised citizens. Dalmatians had to own at least £10 before landing in New Zealand.

Later in the 20th century, the wall of prejudice broke up because:

- most Dalmatians moved away from gumfields.
- they turned to other jobs.
- some went to mining areas like Thames.
- some settled on the land as orchardists.
- some started up restaurants.
- some started up the New Zealand wine industry.
- people learned to admire the Dalmatian energy and the way they worked in groups.
- people realised Dalmatians were not going to ruin the country.
- people lost their fear of them.
- most Dalmatian families were here to stay.
- they stayed in New Zealand because of the long distances home, the lack of jobs back home, and the opportunities in New Zealand.
- they helped develop New Zealand economically.
- people realised Dalmatians were not going to take over the whole country despite their big numbers.

Activities

1 Discuss the pushing factors of Dalmatian immigration (why they wanted to leave), and the pulling factors (why New Zealand attracted them).

2 A fact is something that is true and can be proved. An opinion is not necessarily true; nor can it be proved. Make your own copy of the Wall of Prejudice but use only blocks that contain a fact. Explain what has happened to your wall and why.

3 Describe what is happening in the cartoon.

4 Give three dates the cartoon most likely appeared. Explain how you could check to find which date it was.

5 Explain the meanings of phylloxera, Croatia, plague of locusts, Royal Commissions, naturalised.

6 Research: Find out what happened, and why, to Dalmatians in New Zealand during World War 1.

ISBN 9780170182256

Pioneering Females

Focus

- Events have causes and effects.
- People move between places which has results for people and places.
- Ideas and actions of people in the past helped shape society.

Pioneers are the first settlers of an area. Here are some points about the lives of European pioneering women.

When they packed their bags they did not have jeans and T-shirts. Instead they packed layers of flannel petticoats and skirts that reached the ground.

Even when they got to New Zealand, they followed fashions from England. They did however, change the materials. Muslin, linen and duck (heavy plain cotton) became popular.

She might have a six mile (10km) ride to church carrying her crinoline on the saddle pommel, or a 2 mile (3.2km) hike to a creek for water with a baby on her back.

Or she might have to ride through dense bush across unbridged rivers, leading a packhorse with a child in her arms, another on her back and another on the saddle in front of her.

She might have to hide herself and her children from a Maori raiding party.

In her long skirt and petticoats a woman might have a ten mile (16km) walk to the store to bring 50 lbs (25kg) of supplies home on her back.

Even in the height of summer, females wore their long skirts when they preserved fruit, washed and dried clothes, mended clothes by candle-light, cooked on open fires, plucked poultry and saved the feathers to make a pillow, swept earthen floors and home-schooled their children.

Skirts did not rise off the ground until the 20th century. Some women used a device like a walking stick with a clasp at the end to hold up the hems of their skirt away from mud.

Poor people often made clothes out of white cotton flour bags. However, even poor women would try to have a hat and gloves to wear when going out.

Children were dressed as small versions of their parents. Until the age of three, boys and girls were dressed alike. Boys wore frocks and jackets. At age three they were breeched. This means they were put into their first trousers and their hair was cut. Girls, as well as boys, got into the habit of going bare feet, especially out of town. Girls wore ankle-length dresses. They did not wear trousers.

Women were doctors, house-wives, and mothers to their own families. They were also midwives and nurses to other women and their families.

Husbands were often away on contract work or military duty. Women therefore had to do the farm-work.

Even wealthy women who were used to having servants, had to do many things that servants normally did. This was because many single girls who came to New Zealand as servants got married instead. Later they preferred to work in shops and factories than as servants.

ISBN 9780170182256

Last century's fashions

1840s

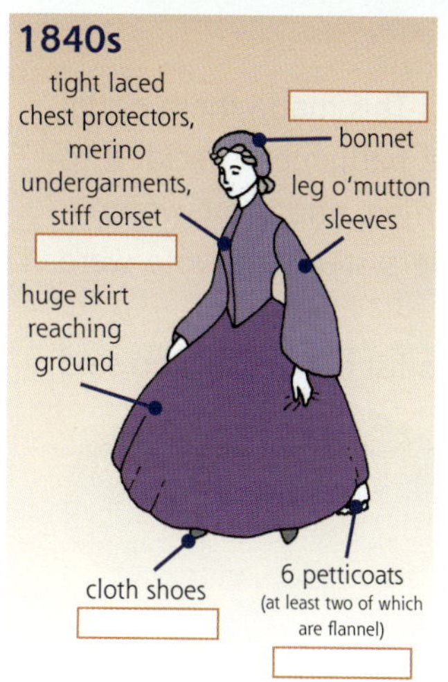

1850s

1860s

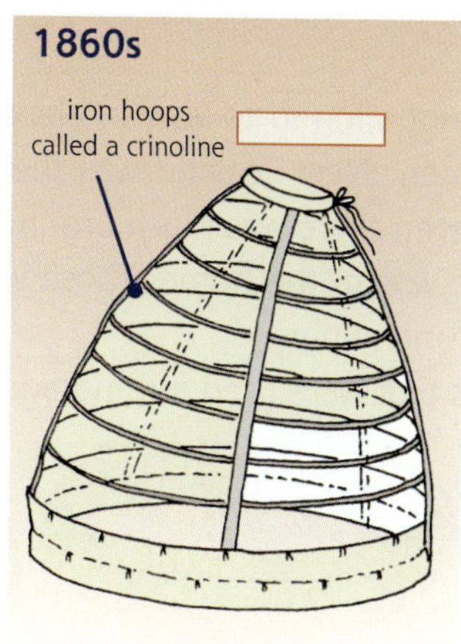

1870s

1880s

1890s

1900s

1910s

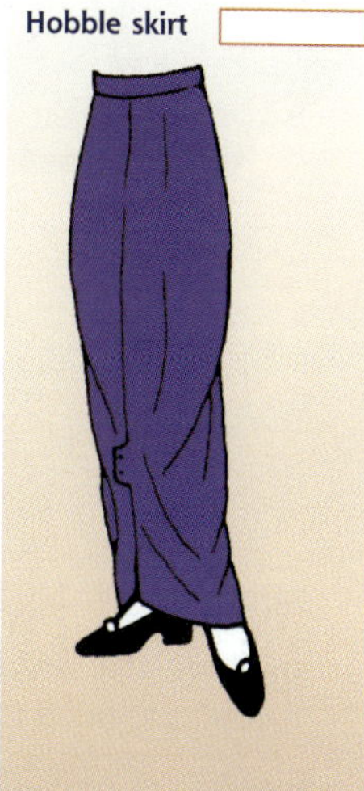

Activities

1 Sketch each fashion. Into the boxes put the missing descriptions from the following:
   - gives some protection from mud
   - show she is moral
   - used to hold balls
   - will have to pin these together to ride a horse
   - takes long time to wash and dry
   - so big a tray can sit on it
   - quickly ruined on mud tracks
   - causes problems on footbridges when rails have to be removed so she can pass
   - a large veil has to be wrapped round this to keep it on when she rides in the first car in the country
   - although these cause headaches and chest problems and swooning, they show she is an upright woman
   - makes walking difficult,
   - shows she is very modest
   - working females wear dark colours and wealthy women wear light colours
   - shows she is a working woman
   - stops her showing ankles while bathing in the sea.

2 Choose one of the fashions and describe how easy or hard it would be to wear.

3 Explain why it was females who followed fashions from Europe yet it was females who had eventually to make the most changes to their clothes in the new country.

4 Research: Find out when females started wearing jeans and long pants.

ISBN 9780170182256

17

Women Win the Vote

Focus

- Events have causes and effects.
- People move between places which has results for people and places.
- Ideas and actions of people in the past helped shape society.

Until 1893 women were not allowed to vote in elections for who got into parliament. This made them equal with lunatic and criminal men. New Zealand was the first country in the world whose parliament decided to give women the vote. However, there was much argument before this happened. Many men, and some women, thought the woman's place was in the home. Those women who wanted to change the system and vote were thought to be freakish and unfeminine.

Here are some arguments that were used for and against giving women the vote and a list of people who said them.

A — Women will vote to stop the liquor trade.

B — Females have done as much as men to settle New Zealand.

C — Political arguments in the home will cause misery, deserted husbands and neglected babies.

D — It is against all womanly modesty to want to vote in elections.

E — A man just out of prison can vote, but his wife, who has not been to prison and looked after his children, can not.

F — Women will be insulted at the polls. Men who want to give females the vote are weaklings and are being bossed by petticoats.

G — It will mean the laws of the country will become more humane (caring).

I — It will get rid of the riots and rowdiness at polling booths.

J — Women who want to vote are a shrieking sisterhood who are going against the Bible.

K — Imagine a tired man coming home from the office to find his parlour full of noisy women talking politics.

Charles is a sheep farmer with his own run. He favours borrowing from overseas to build roads and railways.

Alfred is an MP who expects his wife to host dinner parties and provide peace and order in his home. He never discusses his work with her.

Charlotte is the wife of a wealthy merchant. Her main interests are going to social functions such as balls and keeping up with the latest fashions.

George is a banker. He disapproves of women working in factories and has brought his daughters up to obey their future husbands. His word is law in his house and he calls his wife Mrs.

Mary is 83. She has been religious all her life and objects to modern hymns being sung in church. None of her six daughters got much education.

Will is a bushman who has had no schooling. He believes females are fragile and weak and need protecting.

Katherine is the well-educated wife of a doctor. She has always been interested in the welfare of women and their equality with men.

Thomas is an MP who is interested in welfare laws, pensions and labour laws.

Anne is a factory worker who lives close to a polling booth.

Robert is an MP with a strong sense of fairness. He encourages his wife to have outside interests and discusses politics with her often.

Harry is a bachelor who owns a successful hotel. He has plans to buy a second one.

Settlers from Britain brought their social ideas with them and that included the idea that the female's place was in the home, not in a polling booth.

Women vote at their first election at Tahakopa.

ISBN 9780170182256

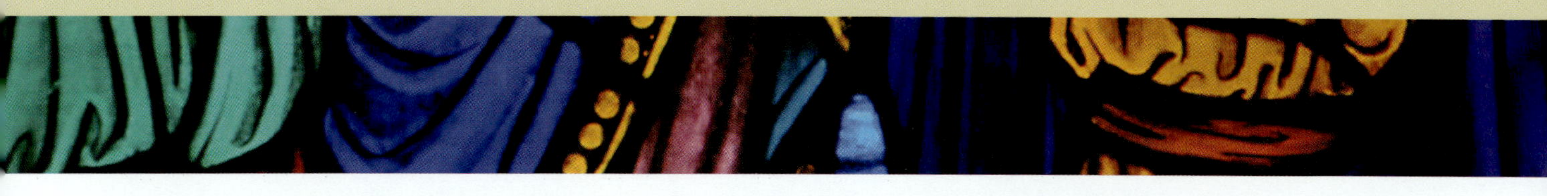

In 1978 a law called the Human Rights Act made it illegal to discriminate against anybody because of their sex. The W shape shows some of the 'Firsts' for females in New Zealand.

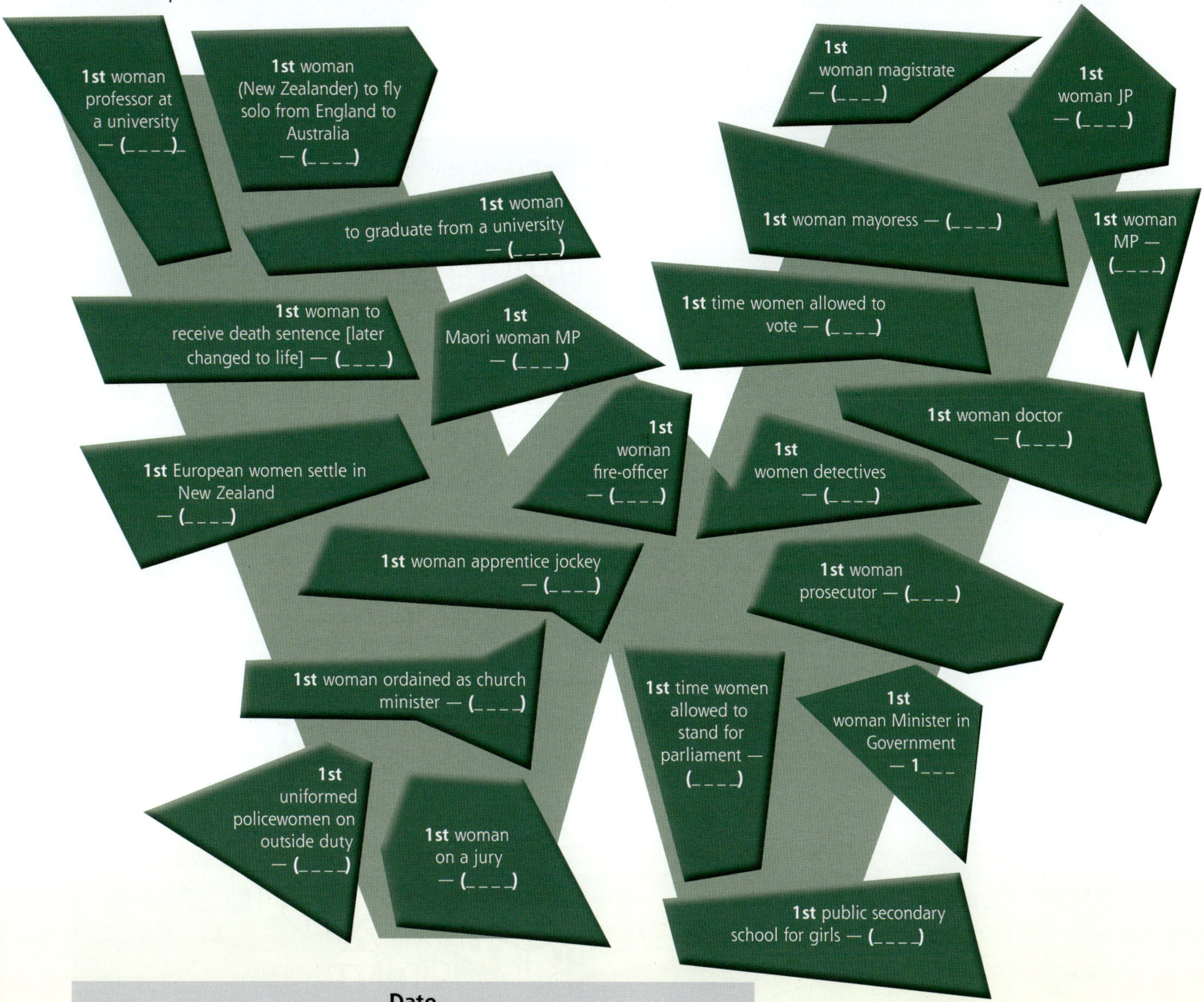

1st woman professor at a university — (____)

1st woman (New Zealander) to fly solo from England to Australia — (____)

1st woman to graduate from a university — (____)

1st woman to receive death sentence [later changed to life] — (____)

1st Maori woman MP — (____)

1st European women settle in New Zealand — (____)

1st woman fire-officer — (____)

1st woman apprentice jockey — (____)

1st woman ordained as church minister — (____)

1st uniformed policewomen on outside duty — (____)

1st woman on a jury — (____)

1st time women allowed to stand for parliament — (____)

1st public secondary school for girls — (____)

1st woman Minister in Government — 1___

1st woman prosecutor — (____)

1st women detectives — (____)

1st woman doctor — (____)

1st time women allowed to vote — (____)

1st woman MP — (____)

1st woman mayoress — (____)

1st woman magistrate — (____)

1st woman JP — (____)

Date					
1814	1871	1872	1877	1893	1893
1897	1911	1919	1926	1933	1934
1943	1947	1949	1949	1958	1959
1972	1975	1977	1977		

Activities

1 Match each argument to a person about women getting the vote. Explain why you chose each combination.

2 Choose one argument and prepare a few more sentences on it.

3 Make your own copy of the W shape. Your puzzle pieces will fit on this. Make your own copy of the puzzle pieces and cut them out. Arrange them on your W shape and attach. Use the dates to fill in the brackets starting from the left top and finishing at the right top. Make up a suitable title for your finished shape.

4 Research: Find 5 to 10 resources about how females have contributed to shaping society in New Zealand.

ISBN 9780170182256

Hard Work and Worry

Focus

- Events have causes and effects.
- People move between places which has results for people and places.
- Ideas and actions of people in the past helped shape society.
- Economic decisions have an impact on people and communities.
- The way people manage resources has an impact on the environment.

You are the wife of a sheep farmer in 1868. Your days are filled with work and worry which always seem to be chasing you. The map shows your house and environment.

Sheep Station
House
Lake
Mountains
River
Ford
Track of 10 miles (16 km)
Limeworks
Birch Trees
Saw Mill
Wharf
Paddle Steamer
Immigrant house for new arrivals
Fell Mongery for tanning hides
Timber Yard
Bakery
Brewery
General Store
Water Powered Flour Mill
Town Houses
Lodging House
TO GOLDFIELDS
Church
River
Cemetery
Clay
Brick Kiln
Fish Hatchery

Rules of the Chase Game

You will need two markers – Wife and Work & Worry. Make these out of paper. Spin a coin for moves. Heads = 1 space, tails = 2 spaces. Wife goes first. Work & Worry tries to catch Wife by moving into the same space. Wife is also caught if she lands on the same space as Work & Worry. Each time Wife is caught she makes a note of it. The winner is the Wife who has done the least amount of work and worry.

Work & Worry

ISBN 9780170182256

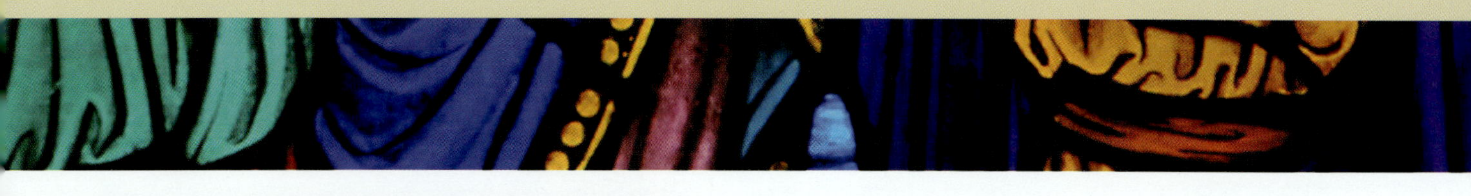

The Chase Game

1

There is no school so you give lessons to the eldest children. You teach them to save everything, even apple pips to plant again.

2

You are worried about your husband and sons who are out snow-raking for sheep after a big snow-storm. More blizzards are expected and you fear the house roof might collapse.

3

Your eldest son drowns on the lake when an unexpected storm overturns his boat. A second son survives but you have to nurse him back to health for several months.

4

A minister brings news of Maori dying of disease in the only pa in this area. You go to help nurse them and stay for a week until exhaustion and your own ill-health force you home.

5

A storm blows the chimney down. You have to make a calico lean-to in which to cook until the chimney is fixed. All cooking is in saucepans and camp oven. Your diet is mutton, damper and home-made bread.

6

A miner is on the doorstep demanding liquor. When you refuse he becomes threatening. You get the gun and order him off. You hide the smallest children in a cupboard in case he returns.

7

You pickle, preserve and salt mutton. When the yeast for bread-making does not rise because of the cold you have to start again. As a treat for the children you use brown sugar to make doughboys and a roly poly.

8

A child from another station arrives in the middle of the night asking for help. You take a hurricane lamp and go on horseback. You stay all night with the sick mother and three children with diptheria. You save two children but one dies.

9

There are heavy snows and hard frosts. Liquid is frozen solid in jugs. You have to cut extra firewood to keep the fire big for warmth and cooking. You suffer greatly from loneliness and have nothing to read but The Bible and *Pilgrim's Progress*.

10

You have another baby. You send your husband for the howdie. There are no anaesthetics or medical supervision. The howdie is too late for the birth but stays for 3 days to help with housework.

11

On wash day and family bath day you have to heat water over the fire. You hang clothes around the fire for drying. Your husband warns you to keep an eye open for a wild boar that has caused much damage.

12

You are running short of provisions but wool prices are low so you have to cut down on what you order from town. This means much extra sewing, mending and cooking. You make clothes for the family by hand.

13

You sit up all night with a sick child feeding her castor oil and beef tea. She is still ill in the morning but the track out is impassable. You take her in the rowboat to wait for the steamer to get her to a doctor but she dies on the way.

14

A group of starving miners who have got lost, arrive. You make them porridge and soup. They repay you by chopping firewood and fixing the wheel on the bullock dray so you can go and care for a sick shepherd.

15

A thaw with rain and warm winds causes the river to flood the house. You put the children in the top bunks and float a go-ashore with a fire in it from bed to bed to keep them warm.

Activities

1 Find the terms for lumps of fried dough that are now called doughnuts, pudding of pastry spread with jam, place dealing with sheepskins and removal of wool from dead sheep, a book published in 1768 about a Christian's journey, midwife, a big pot.

2 Play The Chase Game twice.

3 Use the material in The Chase Game to write a letter to your grandparents in England. Explain how hard your mother has been working.

4 Create an extra five to ten spaces you could add to The Chase Game but make each something positive for the wife. For example, her husband builds an inside bathroom.

5 Make up a chart to show whether or not, and why, you are likely to visit each of the places marked on the map.

6 Research: Find out how big early sheep stations were in the South Island.

ISBN 9780170182256

Long Journeys to New Land

Focus

- Events have causes and effects.
- People move between places which has results for people and places.
- Exploration creates chances and challenges.
- Ideas and actions of people in the past helped shape society.
- Economic decisions have an impact on people and communities.
- The way people manage resources has an impact on the environment.

The Journey of 1863

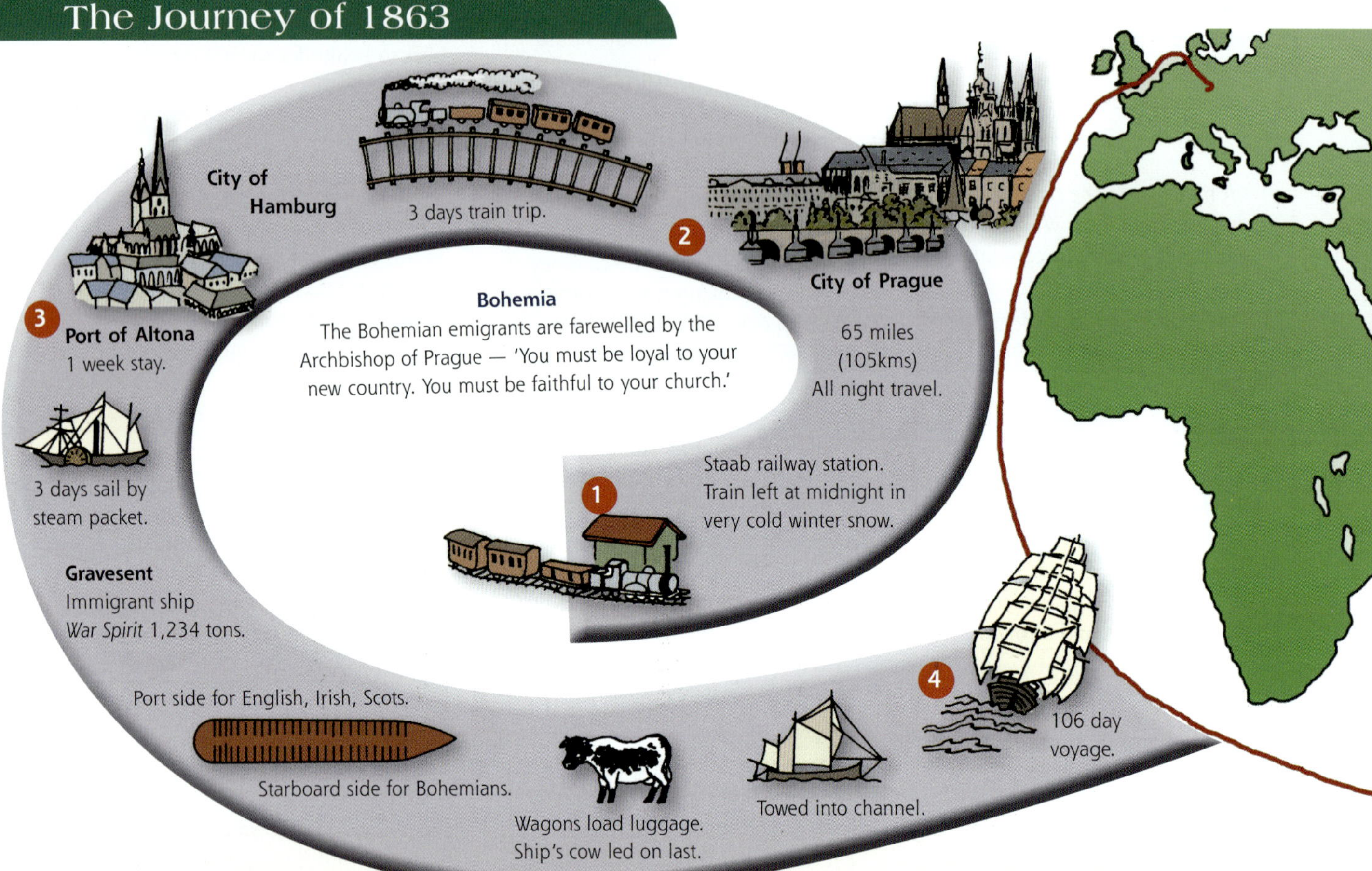

The voyage by ship to New Zealand from a home port was long enough. Many immigrants faced extra journeys before they boarded and when they left the ship.

In 1863, for example, 83 immigrants left a little place called Staab in Bohemia which is today in the Czech Republic. They travelled to the mouth of the Puhoi River in the North Island of New Zealand. Another two groups of Bohemian immigrants came out in 1866 and 1875. The Auckland Council had agreed to give them each 40 acres (16.2 hectares) of land if they paid their own fares. Each child was to get 20 acres of land.

The Journey of 1863 shows the main stages of how immigrants got to New Zealand.

The Bohemians were poor. They had a struggle to survive. To earn money they cut shingles. These were used for roofing. Auckland was 30 miles (48km) away. The Bohemian's cost of sending shingles there was half the price they got for the shingles.

For the men, there was a roadmaking contract for several years. They earned 4 to 5 shillings a day for this. When that ended, they sold fungus from decaying trees to the Chinese market.

How to cut and sell shingles

- Saw tree trunks into short lengths and make them square.
- Put them into a hollow cut into a big log.
- Put a sharp axe on the timber and tap with a mallet.
- Tie the shingles into bundles with supplejack (bush vine).
- Take the bundles on your back to the river. Load them on to a home-made punt and go to the river mouth to wait for the schooner.
- You cannot afford boat fares so you walk to Auckland to sell the shingles.

ISBN 9780170182256

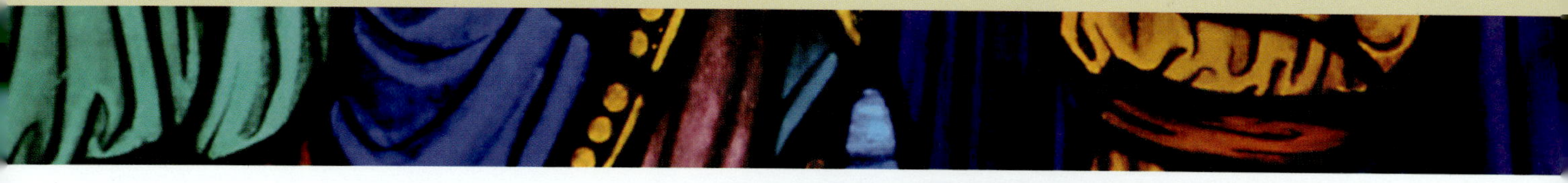

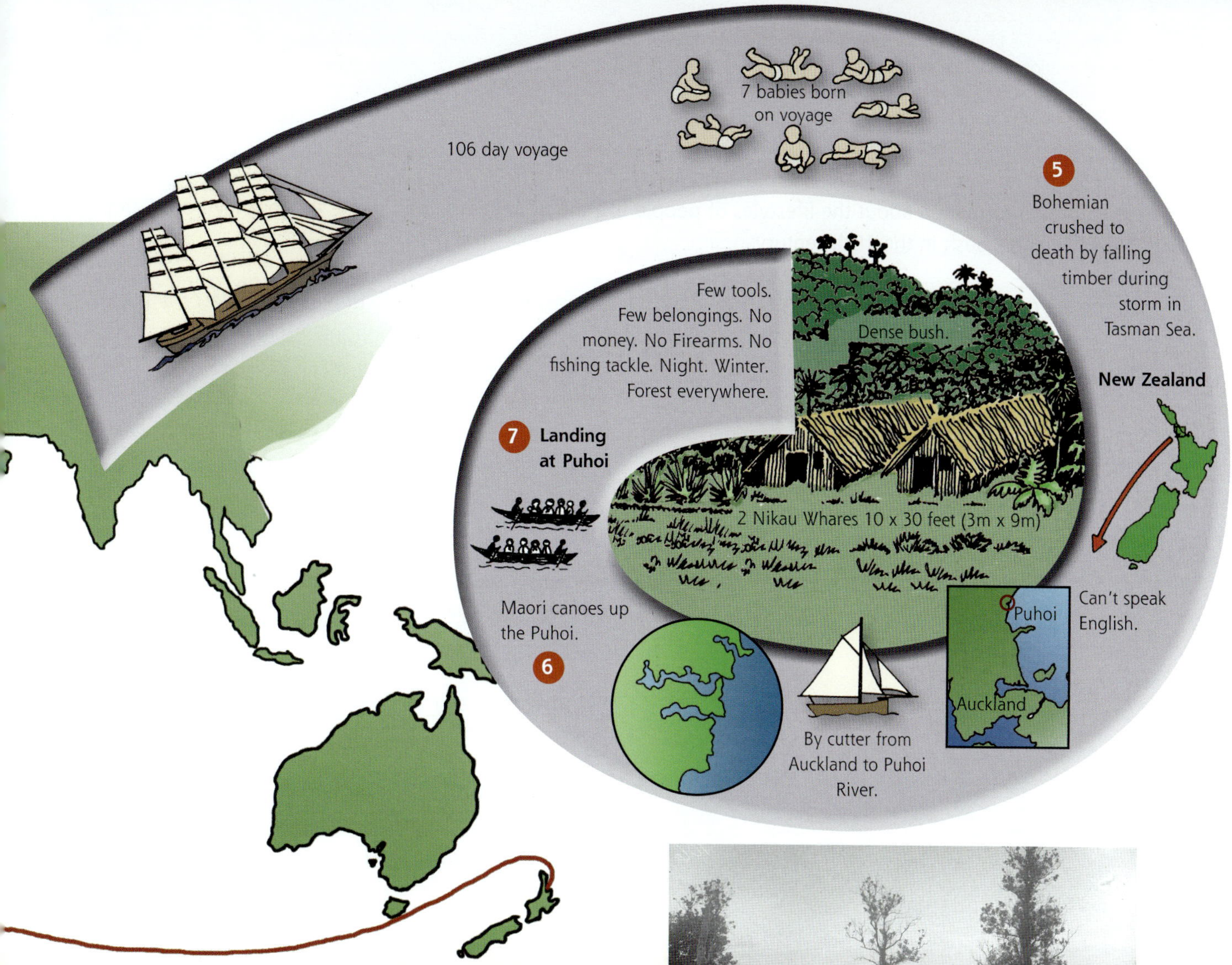

106 day voyage

7 babies born on voyage

5 Bohemian crushed to death by falling timber during storm in Tasman Sea.

New Zealand

Few tools. Few belongings. No money. No Firearms. No fishing tackle. Night. Winter. Forest everywhere.

Dense bush.

7 Landing at Puhoi

2 Nikau Whares 10 x 30 feet (3m x 9m)

Maori canoes up the Puhoi.

6

Puhoi

Auckland

Can't speak English.

By cutter from Auckland to Puhoi River.

Gradually there was enough money for the family to buy a cow. It supplied butter, milk and cheese for their own use and the Auckland market. They could also buy some poultry which gave them eggs to sell in Auckland. If they were lucky there might also be enough money to buy a horse for working and transport.

Activities

1 Make your own copy of the Journey of 1863. Beside each number put one word from the box which might best describe the feelings of the immigrants.

frightened	bored	serious	sad
impatient	excited	disappointed	

2 The top photo shows the area near the Puhoi river mouth some time between 1863 and 1905. Discuss the advantages the area offered the immigrants.

3 The bottom photo shows Puhoi in the early 20th century. Describe how immigrants are changing the environment.

4 Research: Find out what the settlement of Puhoi is like today and if the Bohemian culture is being kept alive.

ISBN 9780170182256

Bush Settlers

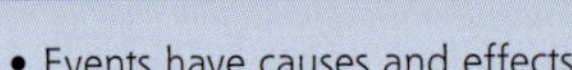

Focus

- Events have causes and effects.
- People move between places which has results for people and places.
- Exploration creates chances and challenges.
- Ideas and actions of people in the past helped shape society.
- Economic decisions have an impact on people and communities.
- The way people manage resources has an impact on the environment.

Here is some information about the lifestyles of people like the Bohemians, who made the journey from Europe to New Zealand's bush in the 19th century.

Clearing your own land: Clear a space to build the house. Clear the rest by cutting down trees and burning undergrowth. Take out as many stumps as possible. Leave the rest to rot. Sow grass in ashes from fires. Put cows in to stop fern growing again. Fence paddocks with post and rail. Put in crops of wheat, oat, maize, potatoes, turnips.

How to make bush apple pie: Gather young fronds of punga fern. Scrape off fur, wash and cut up. Make the pastry with flour beaten with mashed potatoes and water.

Firewood: The house needs a constant supply of wood, even in summer, to keep the fire going for cooking.

How to make flour: Thresh wheat with a hand flail. Grind into flour in a small mill turned by hand.

The bathroom: This is the creek. Giving the family a hot bath is a whole day's work.

Food from the bush: This includes wild pork, bush honey, eels and freshwater crayfish, drinking water, berries, tea made from bidibidi, fern root (washed and pounded, tastes a bit like gingerbread), birds such as wood pigeons and kaka.

Transport: A heifer is broken in to carry a pack. Later a pack-horse is bought. A horse is better than a bullock. In a swamp, a horse struggles to get out whereas a bullock gets suffocated. You can also hang on to a horse's tail to get up cliffs. The nearest town is 26 miles (41kms) away. There is no money to stay overnight. You walk and have a sleep in the bush on the way home.

Outside work: Men are often away from home during the week or for weeks on end. They make roads, make shingles and gather fungus for export.

Houses: Usually a nikau whare or hut built of pit-sawn timber.

Washing clothes: Use the creek. If there is enough money for a copper, water can be heated in the copper over a fire and clothes boiled. They then need rinsing, either in the creek or copper.

The toilet: This is a long-drop.

How to churn butter: Milk cows and strain milk. Scald milk over a fire in a kerosene tin. Pour it into basins. Leave 24-36 hours for cream to rise. Skim cream off with a piece of tin with holes in. Beat cream into butter with a flat stick.

ISBN 9780170182256

Females: They get up at daybreak to do chores so that by 6 o'clock they can take an axe and spade and hack at undergrowth.

Health care: Doctors are usually too far away and too expensive. Tar is used on wounds as a dressing, or cobwebs are packed into wounds. Cuts are sewn up with needle and thread. Koromiko leaves and manuka berries are good to soothe upset stomachs. Sores are treated with mamaku pith and rata sap stops bleeding. Broken limbs are set between boards.

Home-made products: Grated potato dried in the sun provides arrowroot starch to use as a food or food thickener. Coffee comes from burnt corn. Rennet comes from the lining of a calf stomach filled with salt; it is used to make junket. Soap is made from fat and soda. Kauri gum, which contains turpentine, is used to light fires. Pieces of gum wrapped in flax are used as torches. Tallow (fat) in zinc moulds make candles. The lead that tea is wrapped in is boiled in a pot and poured into moulds to make rifle bullets. Bottles with tops taken off make glasses and jars. Clothes are made from flour bags. Newspapers make wallpaper. Grass tied to a stick makes a broom.

Education: It may be many years before a school is built. Children are either home-schooled or get no formal education.

Entertainment: Groups have their traditional musical instruments. An English settler might have a piano. A Bohemian might have a dudelsack. It looks like bagpipes. A church might organise activities such as a picnic. Families might have home-made skittles or quoits. A wedding is a big event.

How to make a dairy: Find a tree with big spreading branches. Split bags and hang them to make walls and a roof. Build a wooden bench rail to hold milk basins.

Female's big fears: Women hated the thought of seeing their children hungry. They worried bush rats might attack their babies. Children could get lost in the bush. Falling trees could kill or injure. A bush fire might spread out of control.

Activities

1 Explain how immigrants did the following tasks – made an apple pie, wallpapered their house, cleared their land, coped without a doctor.

2 Describe how you would use a flail, quoits, grated potato, rennet and tallow.

3 Problem-solve the following:

a) The two eldest girls in the family both want to go to the school that has just opened but the mother can spare only one of them from house and farm work.

b) A fire has been lit to burn some fern. The fire is starting to drift towards the whare.

c) The family has run out of tea, sugar, bullets and soap and has no money to buy any more.

d) A boy has had an accident in the bush. He has broken a leg and badly gashed the other.

e) There are rumours of an escaped prisoner hiding out in the bush in this area.

f) The creek beside the house has dried up but it has just started to rain.

g) The family has found an old Maori canoe but it leaks.

h) The family's two cows have broken down the rails and strayed into the bush.

4 Research: Find out what the European attitude to the bush was.

ISBN 9780170182256

The Prize Was Land of Their Own

Focus
- Events have causes and effects.
- People move between places which has results for people and places.
- Exploration creates chances and challenges.
- Cultural interaction impacts on cultures and societies.
- Ideas and actions of people in the past helped shape society.
- Economic decisions have an impact on people and communities.

In the 1870s and 1880s nearly 8,000 immigrants from Europe were assisted to New Zealand. The main groups were German, Danish, Norwegian and Swedish.

Many of these went to Special Settlements. This was the name given to a contract made to develop an area of bush. The contractor usually had the job of getting immigrants to settle the land.

An example of a Special Settlement is the Scandinavians in the Seventy Mile Bush. Scandinavians were from Norway, Sweden and Denmark. People from Finland and Iceland are often considered to be Scandinavians as well.

The Scandanavians in the Seventy Mile Bush

The Seventy Mile Bush was bought from Maori in 1870. It was nearly 300,000 acres (121,406h) running from southern Hawkes Bay to the Wairarapa Valley. The immigrants walked from Wellington and Napier into the bush.

The voyage from Scandinavia cost £5. The land was £1 an acre. Many of the immigrants had to give I.O.U.s. In Scandinavia they had given up hope of ever getting their own farm. In New Zealand they had to work hard to earn their prize – 40 acres of land for each family farm. There were also many hidden costs before they won their prize.

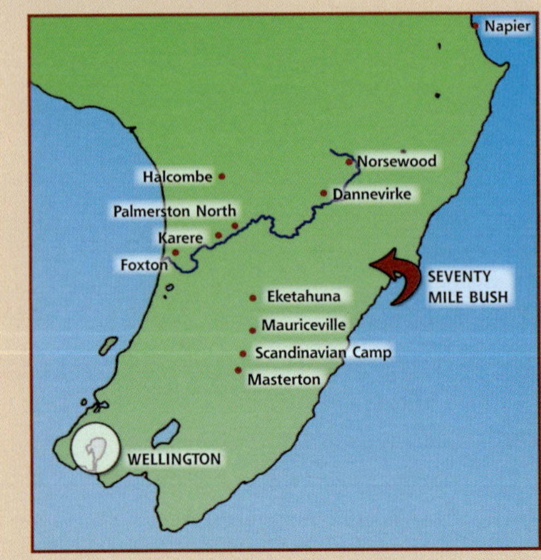

ISBN 9780170182256

Chart 1

1. The journey to their sites takes them through some beautiful bush. Then they see their sections — no clear land at all, no pasture, nothing but bush.
2. Life is all about clearing away the bush.
3. They are shown their first homes — rough barracks with canvas roofs and oiled calico windows. Families with children have two rooms. Married couples with no children have one room.
4. There is no money to buy blasting powder. It is a whole week's work to dig out one stump. Some are too big to dig out. They have to be left for several months to dry before they can be burnt.
5. Men chop down the big trees. Women and children chop down smaller trees and undergrowth.
6. Soon everyone's hands are covered in blisters and sores. They have to wrap old bits of material round their hands.
7. On their own land, the first job is to build a ponga log hut. This is two rooms — kitchen and family bedroom. Windows are oiled calico, roof is fern thatch, and the floor is stamped-down earth.
8. The hut has to have a big fire-place at one end for meals to be cooked in huge pots.
9. They cannot leave New Zealand and go back home because they have no money and cannot speak English.
10. The women give birth, live and work in the bush, cut off from all town life.
11. There is no school.
12. The men are given tools, taken a long way into the bush and shown the area to be cleared for road and rail. When they have finished, they will be able to work on their own land.
13. Many of the men are skilled carpenters and cabinet makers.

Chart 2

- A Not being able to use their craft and training.
- B Feelings of being trapped.
- C Ruined hands.
- D Wife and children have to work and children have adult responsibilities.
- E Feelings of despair.
- F Primitive homes, different to what they are used to.
- G Extra stress on females.
- H Homesickness for Scandinavian foods.
- I No leisure time.
- J Lack of privacy.
- K A long, long job.
- L Having nothing to use but axes, crosscut saws and mattocks (like pick-axes) to cut down huge trees.
- M Children go without any formal education.

Activities

1. Describe the location of the Scandinavian camp.
2. From the map, name the town that took its name from:
   a) George Maurice O'Rorke who helped Scandinavian immigration and settlement
   b) being founded largely by immigrants from Norway
   c) the word meaning Danes' work
   d) Maori for 'to run aground on a sandbank'
   e) John Masters who helped settle working people on the land.
3. The Scandinavian camp had bad sanitation. Diseases such as typhoid killed some immigrants. Discuss how names on a map have hidden stories.
4. Draw and label a home built by a bush-settling family.
5. Match the 13 letters from Chart 2 to the 13 numbers of Chart 1.
6. Research: Find some photos of 19th century bush settlements.

ISBN 9780170182256

From the Netherlands

Focus

- Events have causes and effects.
- People move between places which has results for people and places.
- Cultural interaction impacts on cultures and societies.
- Ideas and actions of people in the past helped shape society.
- Economic decisions have an impact on people and communities.

Two World Wars, 1914-18 and 1939-1945, wrecked the lives of many people in Europe. They welcomed the chance to start a new life in a place like New Zealand that had not been destroyed by war. The wars had also brought New Zealand closer to Europe. New Zealand men and women went overseas as soldiers and nurses. New Zealand food helped keep the British fighting.

Some immigrants came as individuals. For example, some New Zealand soldiers brought home wives from Europe.

Some came in small groups. For example, in the 1920s there were immigration schemes for boys and girls to come to New Zealand from Britain.

Some immigrants came through special arrangements between Governments. An example is the arrangement between the New Zealand Government and that of the Netherlands (sometimes called Holland) in 1951. This agreement lasted until 1993. It was about letting in a certain number of immigrants each year from the Netherlands.

Bombed town in Europe.

Flock House was near Bulls in the North Island. It was a grand three-storey home. Its land was a training farm for children of British seamen who had kept shipping lanes open during WW1 so New Zealand produce could not be captured by the enemy.

Flock House boys	423
Flock House girls	121
Public school boys	645
Church of England boys	494
Salvation Army boys	564
Empire Exhibition scholarship boys	12
TOTAL	2259

Dutch immigrants.

ISBN 9780170182256

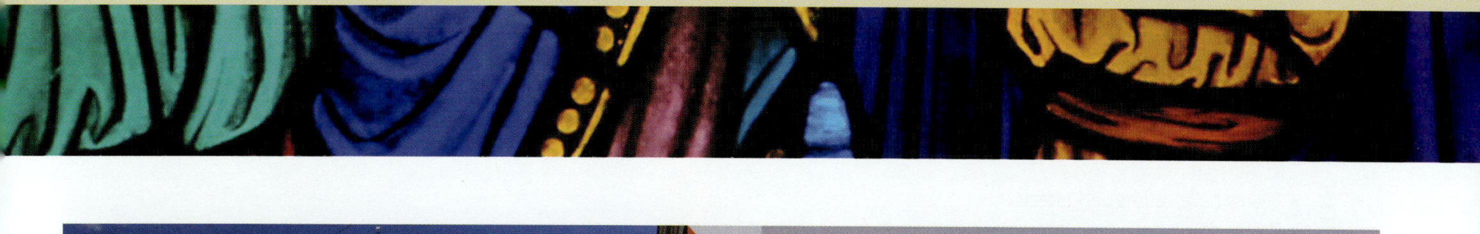

Netherlands

- housing shortage
- job shortage
- over-crowding (ten times less room and ten times more people than in New Zealand)
- had been occupied by Germans during the war.

In the 1950s an average 1806 Dutch arrived each year. Mostly young single men, they were sent to work on dairy farms, and building railways and dams.

New Zealand

- had been far away from fighting in Europe
- good climate
- no great pollution
- Dutch (people from Netherlands) friends and relations already here
- open spaces and freedom
- jobs and houses
- welcomed immigrants from Netherlands as they were European, could fill labour shortages, and were considered hard workers.

Birth places of New Zealand's foreign-born 1961

Italy	1427
Hungary	1496
Poland	2140
Germany	2269
Scandinavia	2507
USA	2616
Yugoslavia	3534
China	4194
Netherlands	17844

Dutch people found Kiwi food strange. They were not used to pies and boiled mutton, and no decent coffee. Because they were non-British immigrants they had to carry Alien Books with their pictures and thumbprints.

Dutch people in New Zealand helped to change features of society.

- good coffee
- Dutch chocolates
- Vogel's bread
- new restaurants
- Lockwood Homes
- Friesian cows
- new ideas on fashion
- photography
- art
- poetry
- architecture
- tulip bulbs (today New Zealand exports tulip bulbs to the Netherlands).

Activities

1 Choose some words from the brackets to describe how the man and the woman in the cartoon are feeling. (proud, uncertain, shy, happy, unhappy, frightened, nervous, worried)
2 Explain why the man in the cartoon is dressed the way he is.
3 Draw a graph for the immigrant boys and girls from Britain.
4 Draw a graph for the 1961 foreign-born figures.
5 It is estimated that 100,000 New Zealanders have Dutch blood. Explain why so many Dutch immigrated here.
6 Explain the link between the flowers and New Zealand and the Netherlands.
7 Research: Find out how the Netherlands got its name, and what it was like at the end of World War 2.

ISBN 9780170182256

Refugee Immigrants

Focus
- Events have causes and effects.
- People move between places which has results for people and places.
- Ideas and actions of people in the past helped shape society.

Refugees are people who have fled for safety to another place. Because they are too frightened to return, they have to find another country to live in. Often, they risk danger and death by fleeing. For example, refugees from South Vietnam were called boat people because they fled in crowded boats and faced ill-health, starvation, pirates, and murder.

There are always millions of refugees in the world at any given time.

Hard core refugees are those who have lived as refugees for a long time or have children born in refugee camps. They may have a family member who is handicapped which stops the family being accepted by other countries.

People who flee their homes and look for refuge within their own country are known as Internally Displaced Persons. There are many millions of these in the world. Once they cross into another country, they become refugees. Sometimes the neighbour country does not want them. So they go to another country. An example is African refugees coming to New Zealand.

Refugees were first distinguished from other immigrants in official statistics in 1944. This was towards the end of World War 2 when so many people had lost their homes or fled their homes in terror of invading soldiers. They often had no identification. In 1950 the International Refugee Organisation issued certificates of identity to Poles so they could immigrate to New Zealand.

In 1944, 734 orphans arrived from Poland. On the Wellington waterfront is a plaque marking their arrival.

Polish orphans.

New Zealand is one of just a few countries that have a refugee quota. This means it takes in a certain number of refugees each year. For example, by 2009 the quota was 750 of the refugees who were waiting in refugee camps or other places to find a new home.

Asylum-seekers are called spontaneous refugees. Spontaneous means you do something without too much thought or planning beforehand. People fleeing their own country and arriving at the border of New Zealand asking to be given safety (asylum) are asylum-seekers. Many arrive with nothing but the clothes they wear, and unable to speak English. New Zealand has one of the highest rates of acceptance of asylum-seekers in the world in proportion to its population.

An immigrant learning to ride bike.

 ISBN 9780170182256

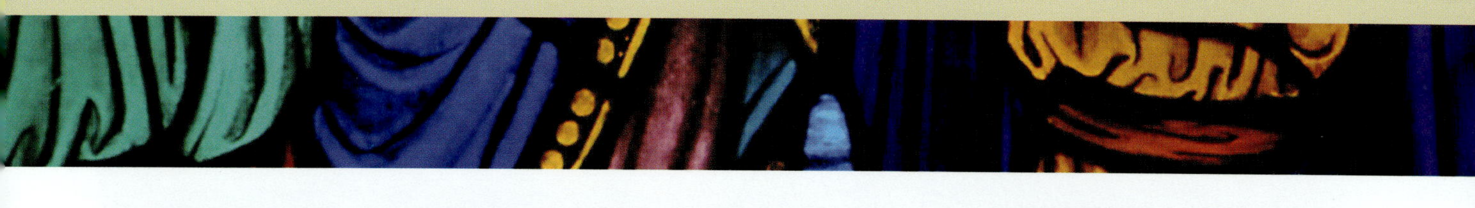

Early refugees went to an immigration camp at Pahiatua. They got an introduction to New Zealand life, culture and language. Today refugees go to a Reception Centre in Mangare for about six weeks. Various government departments look after them. They get a special emergency benefit until the breadwinner starts work. They get warm clothes, medical and dental checkups, language classes. They are also given lessons on how to cope with situations like shopping or calling a doctor. Recent refugees at the Centre have included Afghani, Iraqi, Kurdish, Ethiopian, Somali, Myanmarese, Colombian, Congolese, Sudanese, Bhutanese.

Where New Zealand refugees come from:

- places which are at war with another country eg. Bosnians
- places where another country has invaded eg. Afghani
- places in which two groups are fighting a war (called a civil war) eg. Sri Lanka
- places where there has been a violent uprising eg. Hungarians
- places where disaster or war has killed parents and made orphans eg. Poles
- places where government has expelled a group of people eg. Ugandan Asians
- places where non-Jews attack Jews in pogroms eg. Russian Jews
- places where religious groups are persecuted eg. Iranian Baha'i
- places where disaster such as drought and famine have hit eg. Somalis
- places where government has been overthrown eg. Chileans
- places with economic problems eg. Ethiopians
- places where people are tired of fighting eg. Iraqi soldiers
- places where there is unrest eg. Czechs
- places where climate change is feared eg. Tuvaluans.

Experts say that many millions of people worldwide will be displaced because of climate change. This will cause problems such as rising sea levels, desertification, aquifers drying up, and floods. Already many people have become victims to climate change. Red Cross research shows more people are now displaced by environmental disasters than by war. Such people are called environmental refugees. Victims of political uprisings and violence get help from organisations and Governments. But the world has been slow to recognise environmental refugees. They are not part of official documents like other refugees are. They get no help. Some legal people say that environmental refugees are made homeless by policies of industrialised countries who contribute to climate changes such as global warming. This means industrialised countries are guilty of environmental persecution. And this means the victims should get legal help.

Activities

1 Explain the meanings of aquifers, persecution, climate change, rising sea levels, Red Cross, boat people, quota, spontaneous, Myanmarese, Bhutanese, Pahiatua, Mangare, plaque.

2 As a refugee you have five minutes to pack ten items into a back-pack and flee. Name the items you would pack and the reasons for choosing them.

3 Most non-refugees think that once refugees are settled in New Zealand away from the problems in their home countries, they will be happy. Discuss if that thinking would be correct.

4 Explain the difference between refugee, asylum-seeker, internally displaced person, hard-core refugee and environmental refugee.

5 Research: Find a picture and story of a refugee to New Zealand that you could use in an assignment about refugees.

ISBN 9780170182256

Pacific Island Immigrants

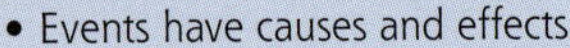

Focus

- Events have causes and effects.
- People move between places which has results for people and places.
- Cultural interaction impacts on cultures and societies.
- Ideas and actions of people in the past helped shape society.
- Economic decisions have an impact on people and communities.

The 1945 census showed that about two thousand Pacific Islanders lived in New Zealand. Today there are more people from some Pacific islands living in New Zealand than there are left on the home island. A recent census put the figure at about 266 thousand which was about 7 percent of the population. One in three lived in Manukau City.

Today's Pacific population is young. Its median age is 21. The median age for the total population of New Zealand is 36. The Pacific population is growing at a faster rate than Maori and European.

Some Islanders come on seasonal work permit schemes to work in horticulture and viticulture. An example is Vanuatuans coming to the Bay of Plenty, especially Te Puke, to pick kiwifruit. Some come back for several years and then become permanent residents. The money workers earn helps villages in their home islands. Sometimes people on work schemes stay past their time. This gave rise to the term 'overstayer'.

Cook Islanders, Nuieans and Tokelauans are New Zealand citizens. This means they are free to enter New Zealand. Other Islanders such as Tongans, Fijians and Samoans have faced barriers to getting in. However, when unskilled labour is needed, the barriers come down.

Pull and push factors for Pacific Island immigration to New Zealand

better medical services	more career choices	excitement of big cities and night-life	better education
over-population	hurricanes	floods	lack of jobs
more money	rising sea-levels	more technology	tropical cyclones
individual freedom	better transport and roads	more sporting opportunities	more democratic government
following family members	political violence such as riots		
not as big as Australia or USA which are other places immigrants tend to go			

Like immigrants from other parts of the world, Islanders often suffer culture shock in New Zealand. This is the term to describe the feeling that everything is strange and confusing. Some immigrants say it is like wandering around a maze, trying to find the exit.

ISBN 9780170182256

The Islanders' maze

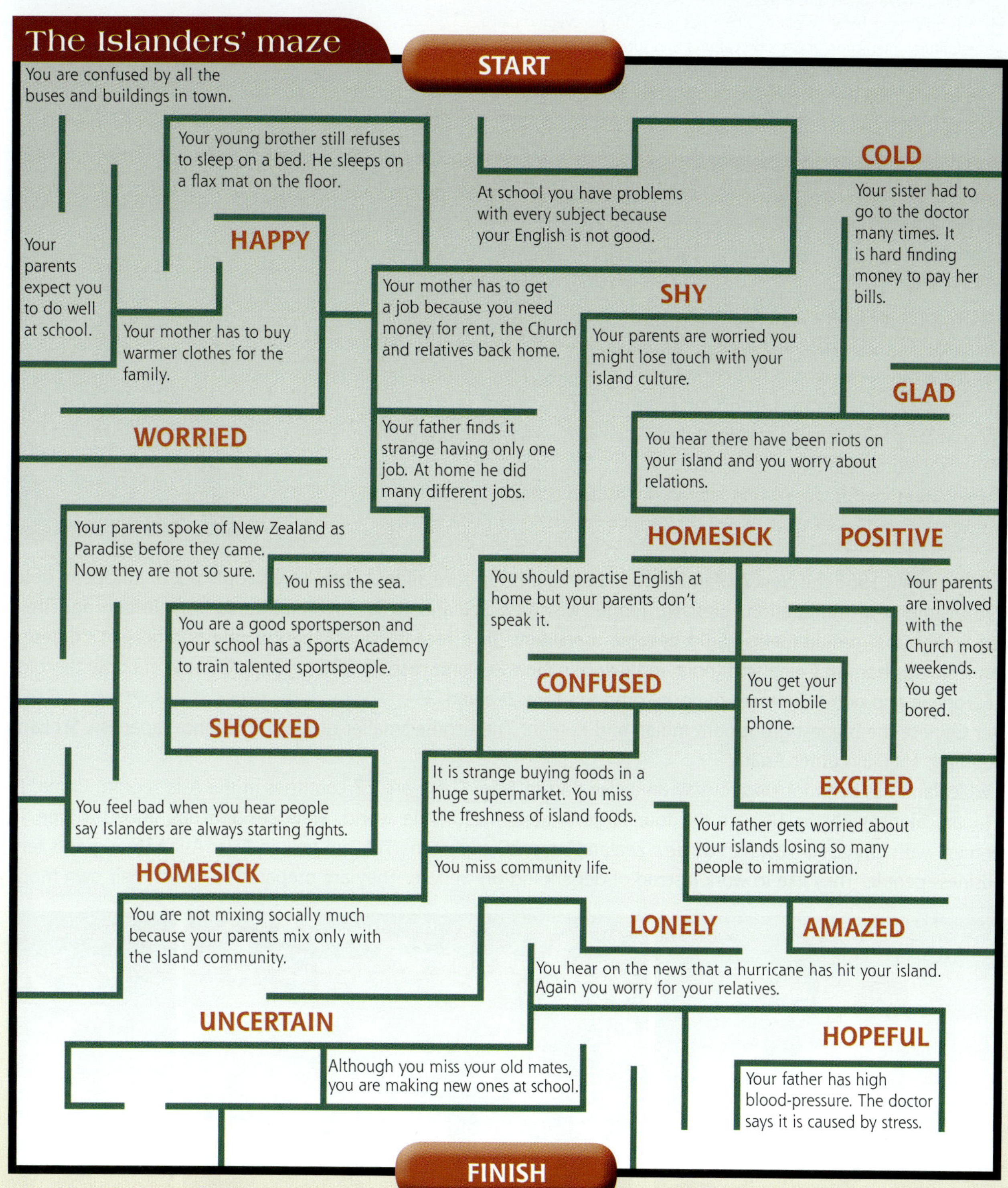

Activities

1. You are an Islander who has been in New Zealand for a week. Use the wrong end of your pen to get through the maze. Make a note of all the things you pass through. Arrange your notes into a paragraph of how you feel as a new immigrant. Use some of the words in capital letters to explain how you feel.
2. Sort the reasons for Pacific Island immigration to New Zealand into push and pull factors.
3. Explain the link between the cartoon (on page 50) and a reason for Pacific Island immigration.
4. Research: Find out about Westfield Style Pasifika, the Pasifika Festival and Pasifika Hotshots.

ISBN 9780170182256

Later Asian Immigration

Focus
- Events have causes and effects.
- People move between places which has results for people and places.
- Cultural interaction impacts on cultures and societies.
- Ideas and actions of people in the past helped shape society.
- Economic decisions have an impact on people and communities.

Asian Entrepreneur (Businessman)

Chew Chong (1827-44 – 1920) was born in China and came to New Zealand in 1867. He collected scrap metal and shipped it to China. In the Taranaki bush he found Jew's Ear fungus growing on some native trees. Chinese used it as a special food and medicine. Chew Chong became a storekeeper. He bought fungus from locals, especially women and children who gathered it. Because it was the main cash income for many farming families, they called it Taranaki wool. Chew Chong exported it to China and imported goods from China. He married a European woman and they had 11 children. His other big economic venture was butter-making.

Chew Chong was the forerunner of today's Asian business people.

For 50 years until 1966 the New Zealand census kept figures for 'race aliens'. They were people not of European descent. In 1987 came new immigration rules. No longer was New Zealand to favour immigrants from Britain and Ireland. Anybody who met requirements could become a resident. In a recent 20-year period, the numbers of Chinese and Indian residents born in China and India and living in New Zealand rose by 800 percent. Chinese are now the biggest non-European and non-Polynesian minority group in New Zealand.

After Chinese the biggest groups are Indian and Korean. Then come smaller groups of Filipino, Japanese, Sri Lankan, Cambodian, Thai and other Asians.

New Zealand has been looking to play an active part in Asia. There are 27 countries in the Asia region. China, India and Japan, along with the US, are the four largest economies in the world. New Zealand has signed a Free Trade Agreement with China. At least half of New Zealand's top 20 export markets are now in Asia. Asian immigrants tend to be business people. They like to work instead of depending on welfare. They are prepared to invest their own money.

From a recent census, Statistics New Zealand said that the four main ethnic populations – Maori, Pacific, Asian and European – would all increase. The Asian population would grow the most. Asian New Zealanders could one day outnumber Maori. At the time, the Immigration Minister said, 'We choose them, they don't choose us.'

Asian immigrants gave rise to terms and nicknames. Astronaut parents are those who work in their home country and the family lives in New Zealand. Cosmonaut couples are those without children who do the same. Parachute kids are those 'dropped off' to live in New Zealand while their parents live elsewhere.

 ISBN 9780170182256

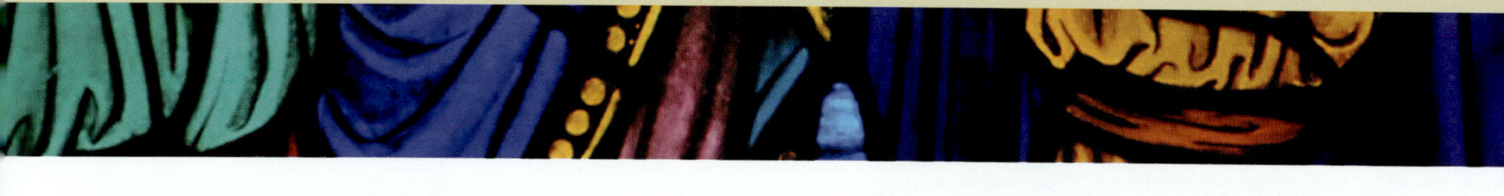

Some pull factors of New Zealand for Asians:

- Safe democracy. No revolts resulting in deaths and harsh laws.
- Wide open spaces.
- Clean environment.
- Stable country. Stands up for issues such as human rights.
- Offers chances for investment for exporting goods around the world.
- Good education system.
- Playing sport is much cheaper than in many Asian countries.
- Freedom of religion.

Asian immigration has often been a polictical issue.

Some minus factors of New Zealand:

- High tax rates and complicated taxation system.
- Distance from home countries.
- Cost of health services.
- English language can be hard to learn.

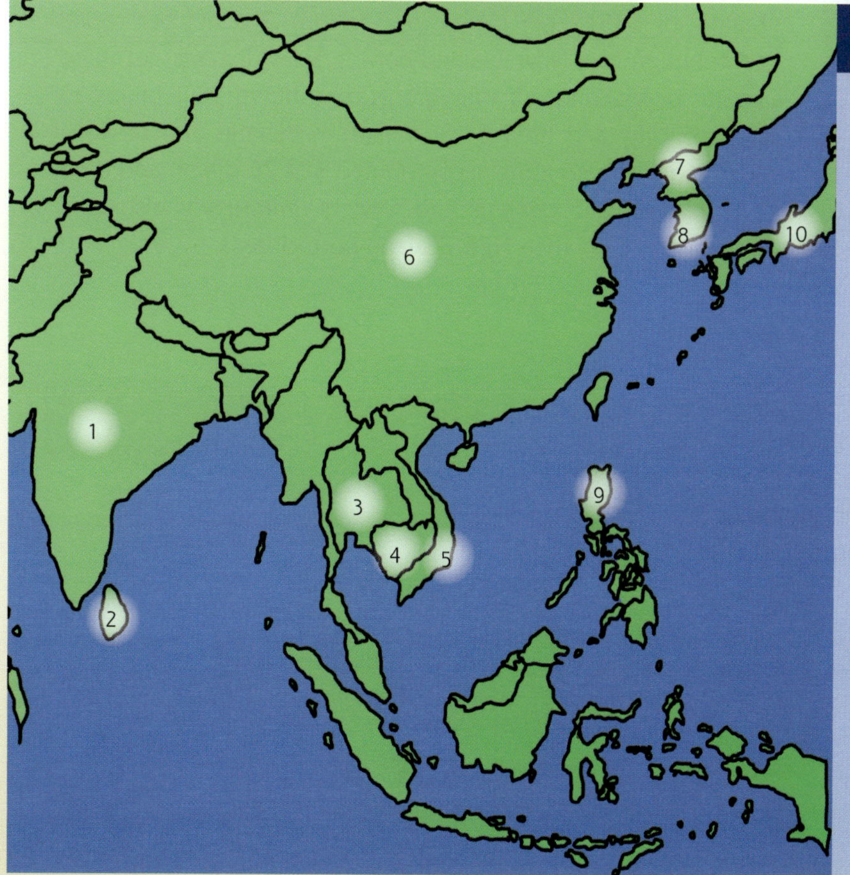

Activities

1. Discuss the impact of Chew Chong on Europeans in his area and the example he set for modern Chinese immigrants.
2. Explain Free Trade Agreement, parachute kids, investment.
3. Make your own copy of the map and write the names of the countries in place of the numbers.

Countries		
China	India	North Korea
South Korea	Philippines	Japan
Cambodia	Sri Lanka	Thailand
	Vietnam	

4. Make up a questionnaire that you could give to Asian students to see which, if any, of the pull factors and minus factors influenced the family decision to immigrate.
5. Explain what the following refer to: 800 percent, 'We choose them', 'race aliens'.
6. Research: Find out about international students in New Zealand.

ISBN 9780170182256

Impact of Tauiwi

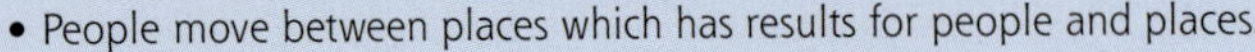

Focus
- People move between places which has results for people and places.
- Cultural interaction impacts on cultures and societies.
- Leadership of groups has results for communities and societies.
- Ideas and actions of people in the past helped shape society.
- Economic decisions have an impact on people and communities.

Immigration New Zealand says immigrants are vital to keep the country running. Kiwis like to go to see the world and immigrants replace them in the workforce. Immigrants also bring overseas contacts to help local businesses. They bring new ideas and new ways of doing things. They add difference and interest to culture and society.

A recent survey showed most immigrants had very good English language skills. About half had an advanced job qualification or university degree. The survey showed the three most common reasons for coming to New Zealand were its relaxed pace of life and lifestyle, its climate or its clean and green environment, and the desire for a better future for their children.

Events in another country often result in a surge of immigrants from that country. For example, the elections in South Africa in 1994 were the first time blacks could vote. The white government lost power. South Africa got a black president. Society changed. South Africans worried about rising crime and future job losses. Many immigrated to New Zealand. It has English as an official language. It has a stable democracy. It has wide open spaces. Its climate is good. It offers jobs.

Most immigrants were white. A few were of mixed race, black or Indian. Soon South Africans became New Zealand's biggest immigrant group after the British, Australian, Samoan, Chinese.

Now New Zealand has South African clubs and churches. Some shops sell food such as bittong (dried meat) and boerewors (sausage). You can listen to Springbok Radio and watch sporting stars such as Irene van Dyk.

Other immigrants arrived with determination to keep ways of doing things from their home country even though New Zealand was a different environment. An example was the English fondness for the sea. In the 19th century English people were horrified at the sight or even thought of human skin being on display. A day at the seaside meant taking in the sea-air as you strolled fully-clothed along a pier. They brought these attitudes with them to New Zealand. Children were sometimes allowed to paddle. The few brave adults who did the same received frowns and scornful looks. If you wanted a swim you had to wait until everyone went home. Or you could use a bathing machine. This was a small enclosed wagon. A horse pulled the wagon into the sea. Inside the wagon you got into your togs. The horse turned around so the back door faced the sea. Down a ladder you went and then into the sea. After your swim you climbed into the wagon and got dressed.

Immigration is always a hot issue in New Zealand. Some people say immigrants do not contribute to the economy. Recent studies show the net impact for having immigrants here is $3.29 billion, or $3547 per capita (per person). The net per capita contribution of a New Zealand-born is $915. Experts got these figures by working out immigrants contributed $8.1 billion to the economy and used $4.81 billion in benefits and services. New Zealand-born citizens contributed $24.76 billion and used $21.92 billion in benefits and services. Immigrants also paid more income tax than New Zealand-born citizens.

Bathing machines on a New Zealand beach.

ISBN 9780170182256

Some Tauiwi arrived with a burning desire to set up a system that was different to one they hated in their home country. For example, John McKenzie was Minister of Lands in the late 19th and early 20th centuries. As a child in Scotland he had seen wealthy landlords throw poor people off land. He was determined to break up vast sheep-runs in New Zealand and let poorer settlers buy small farms.

Experts say that New Zealand's economy could be headed for melt-down if immigration numbers drop. New Zealand has an increasingly greying population. Births alone can not fill gaps in skilled labour.

Check out the news for any day and there is bound to be a story showing an impact of immigration. Here are two from a recent day chosen at random.

A large park in Manukau was officially opened. The opening event was called DiverzCity. It celebrated the range of cultures of Flat Bush and Manukau. It included a Korean break-dance group, a local hip-hop crew, Irish dancers, ethnic food and a cultural market.

The second story was about migrant workers. Many had sold up in their home countries on the promise of a work-to-residence visa. They had heard Government planned to slash work permits. At the same time the Immigration Department was investigating a case of 28 workers in New Plymouth. The workers were made redundant (lost their jobs) while Filipino welders kept their jobs and had temporary permits renewed. The Department was also checking a Hamilton company which had laid off 28 Kiwis while keeping on 24 migrant workers.

Activities

1 List the ethnic groups represented in your class. Explain why your list would be of interest to a social historian in the future.

2 State five facts about this graph.

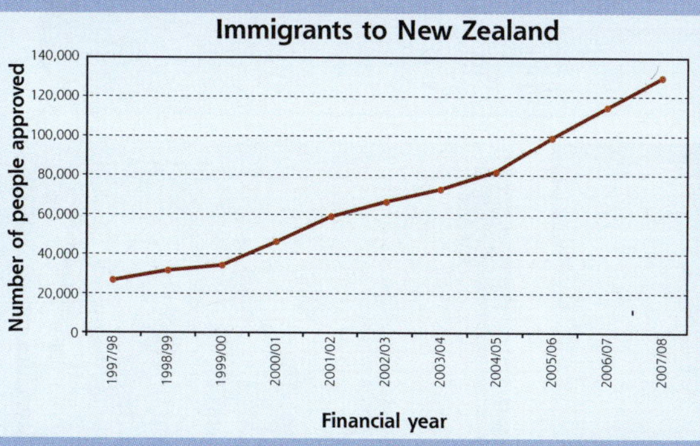

3 Describe what is happening in the cartoon and who the people are.

4 Discuss which has been the main Tauiwi culture in New Zealand. Give at least five reasons for your choice.

5 Run an Artefact Day. This is when students bring artefacts (items from a culture and often from the past) to class and explain what they are. You could vote for the most interesting.

6 Research: Find the graphic that you like best about Tauiwi. Here is one from the 1890s that a student who is a cyclist might choose.

27

Enquiry About Early Tauiwi In Your Local Area

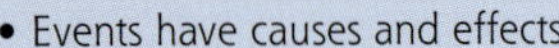

Focus

- Events have causes and effects.
- People move between places which has results for people and places.
- Exploration creates chances and challenges.
- Ideas and actions of people in the past helped shape society.
- Economic decisions have an impact on people and communities.
- The way people manage resources has an impact on the environment.
- People remember and record the past in different ways.

Your local area might be a settlement, town, suburb or city. No matter where you live, whether it is in a sixth-storey apartment or a lighthouse, your local area is full of history. For example, who built your apartment? Who were the first people in your lighthouse?

Think about the classroom you are sitting in right now. At some time in the past, somebody decided to build the school there. Why? Finding answers to such questions is called carrying out an enquiry.

In some places, you have to dig for information about Tauiwi in your local area. In other places it is closer to the surface. Here, for example, are murals on shops in the main street of Katikati. It was a Special Irish Settlement of the 19th century.

Research Activities

1 Make up six questions to form your enquiry about early Tauiwi in your local area. You could use Who, What, When, Where, Why, How. These questions are called focusing questions because they help you to focus your enquiry.

2 Make a plan for your enquiry. For example, how much time you have, the tasks you will do, where you will find information, how you will organise your information.

3 Gather information to answer your six questions. Choose the information that is the most helpful. It might include photographs, a taped interview, a map.

4 Write up your enquiry.

Extra

Draw up a walking tour of places of historical interest in your area.

ISBN 9780170182256